Praise for *Wildeana*

'*Wildeana* is an intriguing, entertaining miscellany of recollections, letters, descriptions, skits, about Oscar Wilde by his contemporaries, as well as scraps of his own writing. An enlightening collection, perfect for dipping into, for Oscar Wilde fans and newcomers alike'

Tatler (Autumn books roundup)

OSCAR WILDE (1854–1900) was born in Dublin. He attended Trinity College Dublin, and – later – Magdalen College, Oxford. During a life crowded with incident he achieved great success as a playwright, and fame as a wit.

MATTHEW STURGIS is the author of *Oscar: A Life* – hailed as 'simply the best modern biography of Wilde.' He has also written acclaimed lives of Aubrey Beardsley and Walter Sickert, as well as *Passionate Attitudes* – a history of the English Decadence of the fin-de-siècle. He has been described – by A.N. Wilson in the *TLS* – as 'the greatest chronicler of the 1890s we have ever had.'

WILDEANA

Oscar Wilde

*Selected with an introduction
by Matthew Sturgis*

riverrun

First published in Great Britain in 2020 by riverrun
This paperback edition published in 2022 by

riverrun

an imprint of

Quercus Editions Ltd
Carmelite House
50 Victoria Embankment
London EC4Y 0DZ

An Hachette UK company

A CIP catalogue record for this book is available from the British Library.

Paperback ISBN 978 1 52940 674 0
Ebook ISBN 978 1 52940 672 6

10 9 8 7 6 5 4 3

Typeset by CC Book Production
Printed and bound in Great Britain by Clays Ltd, Elcograf S.p.A.

Papers used by Quercus are from well-managed forests and other responsible sources.

PREFACE

OSCAR WILDE ARRIVED IN London in 1879, after an impressive undergraduate career at Oxford, with a clear, stated ambition: to win 'success, fame, even notoriety'. And, remarkably, he achieved his goal. Within two years it could be said of him that he was 'more talked about and paragraphed than any other male individual not being a murderer or a statesman'. He was an early example – perhaps even the first – of someone who became famous for being famous. His actual achievements – the charming fairy stories, the brilliant essays, *The Picture of Dorian Gray*, the society comedies, *The Ballad of Reading Gaol* – came later – and so did his real notoriety: the 1895 trials, the two years' imprisonment, the solitary exile, and the death in 1900, at the age of just forty-six.

Early fame ensured that, throughout his life, he was written about by many of those whom he met. And he met everyone. His actions, his manners, his mannerisms, and (above all) his sayings were diligently set down. Wilde's first reputation was as a wit: a sayer of smart things. From his last days at university he was celebrated – or mocked – as master of the ingenious epigram, the provocative paradox, the witty aside, or the extravagant conceit. And it was a reputation that endured. Indeed, even after his literary successes in the 1890s, it remained a common trope that, however sparkling his writings might be, they were but pallid reflections of his verbal exuberance and wit – or ingenious vehicles for the same.

For, if others recorded his conversational flights, so too did Wilde. He used, and re-used, many of his sayings in his published works – in his two great 'duologues' ('The Decay of Lying' and 'The Critic as Artist'), in his one novel, in his four plays, and in the several epigrammatic manifestos that he contributed to the periodical press.

There have, over the years, been many anthologies of Wilde's aphorisms. Indeed he, together with his wife, Constance, was responsible for the first collection – called *Oscariana* – which was privately published by their friend, Arthur Humphreys (of Hatchards) at the beginning of 1895, shortly before the debacle of his trials and disgrace. Since then the process has never ceased. Amongst the most recent gatherings is a small paperback volume put together by Wilde's grandson, Merlin Holland. These works have tended, reasonably enough, to draw on the same rich vein of published material. Certainly, over the decades a definite canon has emerged. The same epigrams have become fixed – repeated, reordered, re-enjoyed.

A similar process has obtained in relation to anecdotes *about* Wilde. There are many of them. In the years immediately following his demise, when his name was still taboo in polite circles, memoir-writers, even those who had known him well, might be cautious about advertising the connection. But the moment was brief. Indeed it can seem that few are the memoirs of the period that do not include some reference to Wilde, or some story about him. Nevertheless, within this great body of material, a canon too has been established.

There have been several influential publications. In their pioneering 1936 volume *Oscar Wilde Discovers America*, Lloyd Lewis and H.J. Smith brought together a wealth of material (press reports, interviews, eye-witness accounts) of Wilde's year-long sojourn in North America during 1882. And this, more recently, has been supplemented by *Oscar Wilde in America: The Interviews* (edited by Matthew Hofer and Gary Scharnhorst), which offers full transcripts of some of Wilde's encounters with the American press. In 1979 E.H. Mikhail put together a magnificent two-volume compendium of *Oscar Wilde: Interviews and Recollections*, drawing together many published accounts of Wilde, extracted from the memoirs of friends and contemporaries. They are invaluable resources for anyone interested in Wilde. But, as with the great anthologies of Wilde's wit, the very excellence of these publications can lead to a false sense of completeness.

I became aware of this while researching my 2018 biography, *Oscar*. In nearly every major archive of Wilde material, I would come across a sheet or two of foolscap in Wilde's distinctive 'Greek and gracious' handwriting, setting down a series of unfamiliar epigrams – unpublished try-outs. Perhaps he had used them in conversation – before, or after, writing them down. Some were certainly adapted, later, into polished lines for plays, or stories, or duologues. Others seem to have been abandoned and forgotten. There were many fascinating new discoveries.

By the same token, a month spent in the stacks of the London Library, scanning the shelves for memoirs written in the first three decades of the twentieth century, brought to light dozens of unfamiliar, and previously ungathered, anecdotes about Wilde: sidelights on his days in Oxford, London, America, Paris, and beyond, by society hostesses, actors, lawyers, men-about-town, minor *littérateurs*, artists, and politicians.

And there were other discoveries. Two previously overlooked letters – one written to Wilde by the Australian-born playwright Haddon Chambers, the other written by Wilde to the editor of *The Sunday Times*, led me to a short story, penned by Chambers, but based on a motif suggested to him by Wilde. It was a striking example – not the only one – of Wilde's amazingly fecund invention as a story-teller being put to use by others; and an example, too, of Wilde's generosity in encouraging the process.

There was a pleasing irony in the discovery of the connection, since five years later, with the triumphant staging of *Lady Windermere's Fan*, some carping critics accused Wilde of borrowing the device of the compromising fan, left in a man's room, from Chambers's recent dramatic success, *The Idler*. And, in a further twist, Chambers's 1900 play *The Tyranny of Tears* was (falsely) rumoured to have been based on a scenario evolved by Wilde during his last days in Paris.

The items gathered here are all small additions to Wilde's story. New tesserae to add to the mosaic – some unfamiliar, others unexpected – they enrich, point, colour and subtly adjust the picture of his life.

Matthew Sturgis

Power was the predominant feature of his personality. At his best he seemed to radiate vitality; and commingled with this was intense charm, but this he was apt to overdo and set one on one's guard.

— 'Wilde's Personal Appearance' – 'by his sister-in-law' [Mrs Frank Leslie], The Soil, *vol. 1, no. 4, 1917*

Scene I: The Poet's study. Lights down. The POET discovered at his writing table L. burning midnight oil. Mysterious music which gradually resolves itself into an Irish jig. To which the POET presently sings:

1.

When first I was hurled on the face of this world
People thought 'twas a thunderbolt fallen.
But when they found who had arrived a Hurroo!
Rent the air – faith 'twas something appalling!
Then a crowd came along many thousand men strong
To gaze on this wonderful child.
For they knew by his cry and the fire in his eye
It was Oscar O'Flaherty Wilde.

Chorus

They may bubble with jest at the way that I'm dressed,
They may scoff at the length of my hair,
They may say that I'm vain, overbearing, inane,
And object to the flowers I wear.
They may laugh till they're ill but the fact remains still,

A fact I've proclaimed since a child,
That it's taken, my dears, nearly two thousand years
To make Oscar O'Flaherty – Wilde.

2.

While at Oxford I took every prize and I shook
The whole College from attic to basement.
When I got up to show them my Newdigate poem
My master was dumb with amazement.
Then he cried, 'I don't need this effusion to read –
I return your MS undefiled.
Your success I proclaim on account of your name,
Mr Oscar O'Flaherty Wilde.'

Chorus

They may bubble with jest at the way that I'm dressed, *etc.*

3.

When I came up to town I soon made a renown,
I dazzled folk with my variety.
Philosopher – artist – and general impartist
Of cynical views of society.
I set London ablaze, and you'll find now-a-days

Aristocracy's tea tables piled
With voluptuous poems bound in delicate tomes,
All by Oscar O'Flaherty Wilde.

> — *The opening of* The Poet and the Puppets, *a burlesque on Wilde by Charles Brookfield, first produced at the Comedy Theatre, London, 19 May 1892, with Charles Hawtrey playing the part of the 'Poet'. At Wilde's insistence, the last line of each verse — and chorus — was amended to remove the specific mention of his name. It was replaced in each instance with the phrase 'neighbour O'Flaherty's child'.*

Height – At least 6 feet (looked even more). Big frame, but well-proportioned. Fleshy and unmuscular and inclined always to corpulence. Head well-poised.

Hair – Not very good natural quality or quantity – of indistinctive brown colour. When worn long (as during American tour) rather straight and lank, to just over the collar; reminded one of the hair of a German professor. Was first curled in the autumn of 1883. Was first cut short and waved in autumn of 1884 . . .

Head – Large and massive (probably took as large a hat as Gladstone). The forehead was strongly pronounced over and between the brows – but fell back above – was low, not high. Great fullness at back of head behind the ears. (He himself favoured the view that the intellectual faculties were not in the forehead, but in the back of the head, and asserted that men of high capabilities had small foreheads.) It was very much the forehead of Irving, for whom he was often mistaken from 1882 to 1883 in the streets of London. (His profile was deep, like Byron's . . .)

Eyes – Pupils of rather a light blue. The eyes were set in a distinct curve in the face. Upper and underlids full – upper lids often drooped over eyes. (Indication of poetical genius.) Expression of eyes – watchful and reflective in one. They were eyes that took note of everything.

Nose – Slender and slightly aquiline. Nostrils rounded, open and sensitive.

Mouth – Lips, pale in colour, large, well defined, but not shapely. Noticeably *flat* and *level* with the *face*, and drawn in at the corners. (I have seen the like lips on persons of undoubtedly scrofulous type.)

Jaws – Long and fleshy, but not ill-shaped.

The whole face, particularly in profile, was suggestive of the more full-faced type of Greek, as seen, not on his statues, but on certain coins or vase-paintings.

— *'Wilde's Personal Appearance'* – *'by his sister-in-law'*
[*Mrs Frank Leslie*], The Soil, *vol. 1, no. 4, 1917*

About Wilde's hairlessness, it struck one as an essential part of his make-up. So far as I can remember it was not due to shaving, but was a natural attribute which heightened the impression of *unmanliness*. Otherwise one would hardly have noticed it.

— *Arthur Shadwell to A.J.A. Symons, 7 July 1931*

Dogmas, for the Use of the Aged

I. The artist is he who can make a beautiful thing.

II. Behind art one cannot find the artist.

III. The critic is he who can write about a beautiful thing.

IV. All criticism is a mode of autobiography.

V. Those who see ugly meanings in beautiful things are corrupt without being charming. This is a grave fault.

VI. Those who see beautiful meanings in beautiful things are the elect. These are not rare.

VII. There is no such thing as a moral or an immoral book. Books are either well written or badly written. That is all.

VIII. The rage of the nineteenth century against Realism is the rage of Caliban on seeing his own face in a glass.

IX. The moral life of man is part of the subject-matter of the artist, but the morality of art consists in the perfect use of an imperfect medium.

X. The rage of the nineteenth century against Idealism is the rage of Caliban at not seeing his own face in a glass.

XI. No artist desires to prove anything. Anybody can prove a thing. Even things that are true can be proved.

XII. To make fiction as lovely as a Persian carpet is the aim of the artist.

XIII. Virtue and vice are to the artist what the colours on his palette are to a painter, what lines and masses are to the sculptor, what notes are to a maker of music.

XIV. Ethical sympathy in an artist is an unpardonable mannerism.

XV. An absolute diversity of opinion amongst critics shows that the work of art in question is rich, complex, and vital.

XVI. When critics disagree, the artist is in accord with himself.

XVII. The highest Art is at once surface and symbol.

XVIII. Those who go beneath the surface do so at their own peril.

XIX. Those who read the symbol do so at their own peril also.

XX. It is the spectator, and not life, that art really mirrors.

XXI. It is not everyone who can be misunderstood. To be misunderstood one must have genius.

XXII. Genius is merely one of the many forms of sanity.

XXIII. Every artist is extremely sensitive to his own praise.

XXIV. We can forgive a man for making a useful thing, as long as he does not admire it. The only excuse for making a thing that is useless is that one should admire it immensely.

XXV. All Art is quite useless.

— *Four MS sheets at the BL. These 'Dogmas' were later amended, and published as 'The Preface' to the 1891 book version of* The Picture of Dorian Gray. *Of the 25 epigrams here, only numbers XX and XXV retain exactly the same form as the 25 maxims in the published 'Preface'.*

The Celts in many things had a strong affinity with the Greeks, the highest honours were given to learning and poetry, and their music had the same subtle power ascribed to the Dorian measure which had 'such strange influence over the human soul, that the bards were often summoned to heal feuds by their divine harmony'.

— *Jane Francesca Wilde, 'The American Irish', 1877*

(Sunday) we drove up to Drogheda, and, under the experienced captainship of Sir William Wilde, entered the subterranean chambers of famous old pre-Celtic kings, perhaps the oldest buildings in Europe, possibly older than the pyramids, of which they are rude types. It was a grand catch to have Wilde – a restless, keen-eyed old gentleman, like a Skye terrier, snuffing and poking about, who has all the district of the Boyne written in the volumes of his brain – as our cicerone.

— *8 June 1874*, The Letters of John Stuart Blackie to His Wife

Under the influence of this father, filled with a passionate love and reverence for the past; under the influence of this mother, enthusiastic over a future for the world which others painted for her, and which she painted for herself in all kinds of marvellous colours; among a crowd of choice spirits, who sympathized with either or both; in the midst of such surroundings young Wilde passed the earliest part of his life, and acquired his early education.

— *'Oscar Wilde's Visit to America'* [*Prospectus published on 24 January 1882, Boston, to publicize Wilde's lecture —* '*The English Renaissance'* – *on Tuesday evening, 31 January, at Boston Music Hall*]

Constance told my wife or me, when staying with us after the tragedy, that he [Oscar] was quite unsympathetic if she referred to the past; he could not be bored with people who go back to their childhood for their tragedies.

— *Otho Lloyd to A.J.A. Symons,* 27 *May* 1937

He says: 'All I remember of O.W. in my childhood days was seeing him dance at my mother's house. We children called him "the wild sheep" because he looked like one! . . . The picture of him when I was a boy of 7 or 8 is vivid.'

— *Edith Somerville (quoting a friend) to A.J.A. Symons, 1935*

Professor Mahaffy, his tutor in Trinity College, made an innings of 65, at a cricket match played with the Viceregal Household, in the Phoenix Park, the day Oscar Wilde transferred his talents to Magdalen College, Oxford, such was *the* Mahaffy's ecstasy at getting rid of a pupil whose lamp was commencing to burn with a ten apollo power, while his (Mahaffy's) stood at number nine.

— Ye Soul Agonies in Ye Life of Oscar Wilde (*1882*)

I remember playing a shocking trick on him at 'Commem' one year. Lunch and tea-parties in each other's rooms were the thing during the week; and he invited to have lunch with him among others Teddy Treffry and his sister-in-law, Baroness [Alice Florence] de Bretton (now Lady Garvagh). I also being of the party, unfortunately arrived first. Oscar had some really beautiful framed drawings on his walls, given him by his friend Frank Miles, of mostly nude subjects; and looking round with an eye to mischief I spotted some penny stamps on the writing table with which I thought it would be a delicate attention to clothe the pretty ladies. This I did, and the party shortly after arrived. First one looked up, giggled and blushed, and then another, till the whole party was convulsed, but all Oscar said to me was 'It's really too bad of you,' but he had to laugh at my inane joke like all the rest. As he never seemed to have devoted any more of his time to work than the rest of us, it came as a bit of a surprise that he took the Newdigate scholarship.

— *Bulmer de Sales La Terriere,* Days that are Gone (*1924*)

[After a picnic, at Blenheim, during Oxford Commem Week, 1877] Gertrude [Ward] and Wilde did not care to pack up the things with us, and so they walked off round a large hay-field. Presently we all began staring at them and laughing, and I heard a great many remarks being made, such as 'Aren't they spoony together?' and a conversation between Mrs Hood and Mr Hilton, 'Do you think it is quite simple?' – 'Oh yes.' – 'Well then there is no harm in it.'

— *Florence Ward's 'Diary'*, 22 June 1877

[At Tegea] in a small room, which did duty for a museum, were collected some more precious relics. Among these were two bas-reliefs of really fine work, though much mutilated. One represented a banqueting scene, in which men and women were arranged in alternate pairs, the men reclining, while the women sat upright. We had some difficulty in seeing these properly, and still more in deciphering a long inscription setting forth the terms of a treaty with some neighbouring State, because the Tegeans of to-day would persist in blocking up the doorway behind us; while faces of every age and description peered in at the one little window which gave light to the room. One of these faces, however, was worth looking at – a nose slightly aquiline, full dark eyes, an olive complexion, overshadowed by a rich waving mass of dark-brown hair. No cameo was ever finer than this face of flesh and blood. Thinking that here at last was the fair Greek maiden we had pictured in our dreams, we looked eagerly round when we came out of the cottage, to find the owner of the face among the crowd. Greatly to our surprise we traced it to an awkward half-grown lad, of some fourteen or fifteen years, who slunk about among his companions as if half-ashamed of his beauty. It was a disappointment; for the character of the face was undoubtedly feminine – and one felt that in a boy its perfect beauty was marred by the lack of strength and firmness. Nevertheless it was a face not easily forgotten.

— *George Macmillan, 'A Ride Across the Peloponnese', in* Blackwood's Edinburgh Magazine, *May 1878.* (*George Macmillan travelled to Greece in April 1877, with Oscar Wilde, Professor Mahaffy, and a young Irishman called William Goulding.*)

20 May 1877

Dear Mr Wilde,

Thanks for your sonnet [on the death of Keats] which is tender and graceful but not true. My life of Keats shows that he was anything but unhappy & he was recognized with unusual rapidity. The medallion is very like him and having been put up by enthusiastic friends it would not do to try and displace it.

I am yrs truly

Houghton

— *Lord Houghton to Oscar Wilde.* (*Wilde had suggested replacing the commemorative medallion of Keats, set in the wall near his grave in the non-Catholic cemetery in Rome.*)

After dinner some undergraduates came in to join the party, and a very tall unusual-looking young gentlemen with longish black hair and a long pale face, very well dressed, was brought up to me and introduced as 'Mr Oscar Wilde'. We spent the evening together but I can't remember much of our talk. I was a very simple unsophisticated girl, and he belonged to a class of society I had never met before. I know he talked about china and I asked him if he were a judge of it, and he said he'd bought a whole service a few days before, and had been taken in. He told me, too, that he was having his rooms decorated, and didn't know what to do about the ceiling, but was thinking of having it gilt. From these memories I gather that he was at that date not entirely artificial and posing, and that in talking to a girl who did not sit at his feet, as some were already doing, he could still to some extent be natural.

— *Mrs Ernest Stuart Roberts*, Sherborne,
Oxford and Cambridge (*1934*)

Methought the day had fallen ne'er to rise.
For in the gorgeous furnace of the west
The long red fires of the dying sun
Had burned away to ashes, and no star
Rose in their place to be my torchbearer:
The tangled silver tresses of the moon
Fell not upon the waters, but instead
Of moon and star and silver netted seas
Did hideous blackness close environ me,
Such as the traveller on Armenian plains
Sees coming from the desert, and straight knows
That he must lie within his tent, and wait
Till night herself, being weary of her reign
Whip on her sable steeds, and once again
The golden waves of morning touch the sun,
So utter was that blackness. Then I saw
One standing by me whom methought I knew,
Or had once known e'er loathly leprosy
Had attended on that bright and boyish face
Which was an angel's once! The horrid plague
Which for the slaughter of the innocent child
Smote Herod, had become his paramour

Kissing his lips with such accursed lust
That they dript bloody poison: whence He came
Too well I knew for the red fire of Hell
Still fought around his body, on his heart
A bloated toad had fed, and such things
Whose father is dead carrion, newt and snake
And cold adder and the churchyard worm
Crawled in and out from vile and blackened holes
Which should have been his eyes. No loathlier sight
Could Virgil show to the great Florentine
In all the wide Inferno. Sin itself
Had shuddered at its handiwork, and all
The foulest fiends who lie in the black pit
Forgot to laugh for horror. With foul hands
And leprous mouth he strove to fawn on me
Whom I in sickened horror thrust aside
And through the shuddering darkness flew away
Whither I knew not, nor indeed did care,
So hideous was this sight which stalked mine eyes
And made my hair stand stiff upon my head
Like rooted spears, so hideous was the form.
But he with squeak such as the bat
Screams when he spies the tawny-breasted owl,
His enemy, so screamed this wretched ghost

Fresh sent from Hell and crying out aloud
'I am thy soul: this hath thou done to me,'
In horrid haste came after: 'O Good God . . .'

— Extract from a long unpublished gothic poem,
in an Oxford notebook

I was very sorry, though hardly surprised at the tone of your letter. Oxford — heaven knows — is an unchristian place enough, but I suppose the atmosphere you live in elsewhere is a hundred times more opposed to the Church. I have somehow the impression that the present was a crisis in your life, and had the hope that even your short visit to Rome may have done something to guide your wandering steps into the Fold. I suppose it was not to be so and that you are content to live for yourself alone, and shut your eyes to the future — as long as you can. It is useless to talk of your weakness and want of principle — truly a strange reason for turning your back on what alone will make you strong (as well might a starving man, on the plea of hunger, stretch out his hand to food) and as for your want of faith and enthusiasm — you cannot pretend to believe that God, who has given you grace to see his truth will not also keep you firm when you choose to embrace it — you *know* He has called you to be a child of the Church, but you are unwilling to give up a hundred and one little sins. It is sheer cowardice, nothing more. It is not even, with you, a question of choosing between two religions, the false and the true. No, you must be a Catholic or nothing. Your choice is between God and the devil, neither more nor less. How *can* you hesitate?

I speak strongly because I speak for the last time. Perhaps I may have said too much already. However the subject is closed for ever between us. But I should not forget to pray for you still.

Do not send me your sonnets. I do *not care to see them*.

The weather here has been horribly cold since I came back, and the change is most disagreeable after Italy . . .

— *David Hunter-Blair to Oscar Wilde, 1 June 1877*

Oscar Wilde had won the Newdigate and was becoming a celebrity. He was introduced to Lily who thought he was silly and affected when he described his idea of what a dinner party should be – 'very little to eat, very little light, and a great many flowers'. We have now less solid food to eat, less light, and more flowers at dinner-parties than in 1878, and I am sure that if Oscar Wilde had looked less queer – he wore a tall white hat on the back of his head and was greenly pale of face – and had been less of a *poseur*, my sister would have been inclined to agree with him.

— *Lady Poore*, An Admiral's Wife in the Making (*1917*)

Lily-like white as snow
    She hardly knew
She was a woman so
    Sweetly she grew.

Had we not loved so well
    Not loved at all
None would have tolled the bell
    None born the pall

She had been . . . . . .

Coffin board, heavy stone:
    Lie on her breast
I vex my heart alone
    She is at rest

Cease cease she cannot hear
    Lyre or sonnet
All my life's buried here
    Heap earth upon it.

> *— Oscar Wilde poetry notebook. (This early pencil version of Wilde's poem 'Requiescat' – which in its final form he dedicated to the memory of his dead sister Isola – suggests that it was originally intended as a lament for a dead lover.)*

Love is always partly a misunderstanding.

Love itself is the worst misunderstanding of all.

Love – a Godlike intoxication; the wine which God gives us to make us greet him on the road.

Life is a riddle and we are always being asked to guess the answer at the wrong moment.

Boys – like postage stamps you must lick them first if you want them to be of use.

— *Epigrams* (*Oxford notebook*)

I saw her thick locks, like a mass
Of honey dripping from the pin,
Each separate hair was like the thin
Gold thread within a Venice glass.

She loosed her pale blue satin stays
She took a carven amber comb,
Her hair fell down like yellow foam.
Or like a sunbeam['s] tangled rays.

— *The manuscript of this poem is included in an elaborately bound
and annotated volume, assembled in the 1920s by a member of
the Douglas family. It has the following (highly speculative) note
attached: 'This poem was written in Wilde's last days at Oxford,
and referred to a woman with whom Wilde was passionately
attached, and probably was the prostitute from whom he
caught syphilis.'*

I saw him in Dublin in the summer of 1878 at a Conversazione given in the room of the College of Surgeons to the British Association. Several notable men were there, amongst them Professor Huxley, and Wilde passed part of the evening with one of Huxley's daughters, a pretty young woman, the same I believe, who later married the painter, John Collier, and ultimately died insane. To her I heard Wilde remark in his airy languid way: 'To think that we are all walking around here, *potential skeletons*!' It may have been here (if the story was true) that Huxley came up and without a word of apology took his daughter away from him.

— *'Stray Recollections' by 'Wilde's brother-in-law'*
[*Otho Lloyd*] *in* The Soil, *vol. 1, no. 4, 1917*

One evening at a dance at a house in Hardwicke Crescent, Dublin, Oscar Wilde danced a minuet with the granddaughter of Daniel O'Connell. When the music stopped he bowed to his partner but with one hand in his pocket. While all the other couples sat down, she stood still, so that Oscar was obliged to take his hand out of his pocket and bow again. He later referred to her as 'a dreadful woman'.

— *O'Connell family tradition*

It had been decided to celebrate the centenary of the poet, Thomas Moore, the author of *Moore's Irish Melodies*. The then Lord Mayor (Sir J. Barrington) lent the Mansion House [Dublin] for the inaugural meeting [in January 1879], to make the necessary arrangements. From this meeting my grandfather, who was the musical adviser to the ceremonies, returned in a fury, complaining of the interference of 'that young vagabond' Tom Sexton, and 'two whipper-snappers', Willie and Oscar Wilde, the two sons of Sir William Wilde, the great oculist. The only cause for 'offence' seemed to be that they had insisted on a better literary effort being submitted for the Celebration 'Ode,' arguing that the one already written by Stephen Nolan Elrington to my grandfather's music was 'not worthy of Ireland'.

— *James M. Glover*, Jimmy Glover His Book (*1911*)

It is very good of you to say what you do about my poor verses – & I like to think that we mutually admire each other – I wish I thought my humble praise could spur you on to really great things, for you, who are young, & above all, a man, seem to me to have before you a 'golden future'. For a poor woman – like me, all I can do is to write passably, considering what I am – & then perhaps people may be astonished that I don't do worse – but you can be anything you like!

— *Violet Fane to Oscar Wilde, May 1879*

Ah what is left for me to do
Whose lips too tired are to sing,
Between the winter and the spring,
Between the old love and new.

— *Oscar Wilde poetry notebook*

Am I asking what it is quite beyond your power to grant in begging you to send an invitation to your ball on the 21st to Oscar Wilde – a Newdigate prizeman & first class at Oxford last year (son of the late Sir William Wilde of Dublin) – a particular friend of ours and a very elegant young fellow, full of love of the arts, and in all respects an accomplished cavalier, who will grace even such a ball, and such a house as yours. I enclose his address on an envelope ready directed and stamped, to save you trouble, for I know you will have more than enough on your hands . . .

— *Tom Taylor to Mrs Boughton, 19 May 1879*

Voice – (light baritone) without a trace of Irish accent or 'brogue', of wide gamut – varied in pace – sometimes hurrying, bright, animated and gay, but more usually measured and deliberate, and even languid (unlike his brother Willie, who spoke very rapidly); its tones were rounded and velvety in character, sometimes slightly throaty and purring; enunciation very distinct and studied; he gave full value to the double letter, in a way unusual in England, in such words as 'adding', 'yellow' etc., and lingers caressingly on the vowels. He spoke with enormous *gusto*, evidently enjoying thoroughly his own imagination and turns of speech.

— *'Wilde's Personal Appearance'* – *'by his sister-in-law'*
[*Mrs Frank Leslie*], The Soil, *vol. 1, no. 4, 1917*

Dear Oscar,

I am <u>so</u> disgusted with myself for forgetting till this moment all about the brougham. I cannot forgive myself so must implore you to forgive me instead . . .

— *Lillie Langtry to Oscar Wilde*

Grey watcher of the starless sea,
Pale warder of the moonless night,
How goes the fiery world with thee
In what fell joys had thou delight[?]

— *Oscar Wilde poetry notebook*

I have pledged myself that you will outgrow your Pessimism and all morbid nonsense, and after your youthful fashionable fermentation come out a clear-headed, vigorous, healthy manly writer. That is the style of man you will meet with us [at the Savile Club] – at least we aim at it.

— *Charles G. Leyland to Oscar Wilde, 4 October 1879*

And she [Agnes Hughes] told me also how one summer Oscar and some other men, one of whom was her young brother Godfrey, went on a bicycle tour in France. Part of the time was very wet and in one small town of the North they came on a melancholy Circus, stranded and draggled in the mud and wet. And they invited the children of the place, and some of their parents too, to the show that night; and scoured the damp countryside to find red roses for the leading lady. And the weather cleared, and the evening was a cheerful success and Oscar presented their bouquet with a courtly bow, and everyone clapped and they left to cries of 'Vive l'Angleterre et vive sa Reine!'

— *C. Hale-White, 'A Tribute to Mark Rutherford'*
(unpublished memoir)

Lady Wilde was immensely tall (I think she must have measured nearly six feet), and her height was emphasized by a most incongruously youthful dress of spotted white muslin, which she wore with a babyish, broad pink sash. I could only think, on contemplating her, of a Brobdingnagian baby! While Lady Wilde was an excellent hostess, and indefatigable in in her endeavours to bring the right people together, she seemed to have no feeling whatever for the personality of her guests, but only for their achievements. This trait was rather humorously manifest when she absent-mindedly introduced my brother-in-law Robert Francillon to his own wife as, 'Two clever people who ought to know each other!'

— *Clara Kathleen Rogers*, The Story of Two Lives (*1927*)

'Chant of the Captive Women After the Fall of Troy'
– from the Greek of Euripides, by Lady Wilde

Strophe

O Breath of the ocean breeze,
Impelling the swift-winged bark
Far over the turbulent seas,
Through the foam and the mist and the dark;
Whither, O whither shall I,
By the breath of the breeze be borne –
To what house as a slave to die,
Or to live as a captive forlorn?

Shall I rest by the Dorian shores,
Or tread the fair Phthian land,
Where the bright Alpidinous pours
His waves over golden sand?
Or sail where the ocean is laving
The isle by Latona trod,
And the palms and the laurels are waving
That sheltered the infant god?

And there with the Delian maidens
By the altar of Artemis stand,
To join in the festal cadence
Of the white-robed priestess band;
Or move in the choral measure,
Though my heart may be crushed by its woe,
The goddess to praise and pleasure
Of the golden chaplet and bow.

Must I watch by the fire of her altar,
Though tears fall fast on the shrine,
And the hymns on my pale lips falter
I breathe to her name divine?
Will she help for my sad entreating,
Or heed the fain suppliant's tears,
While youth with its glory is fleeting
Down the desolate waste of the years?

Antistrophe

The soft lights are dying
Of Asia's loved skies,
And cold winds are sighing

Where pale Europe lies
'Neath her grey ashen shroud,
Wove of storm-wind, and cloud,
And the vapours that veil
Heaven's star-gathered crowd.

We must tread like the dead,
That sad, mist-covered land,
Ever changing and ranging,
A grief-stricken band;
While our bitter tears falling,
Flow fast like the rain,
And no gleams of bright dreams
Ever haunt us again.

Strophe

Shall our home be the olive-crowned city
Where Pallas sits throned in her state,
The victims of wrath or of pity,
The bond-slaves of tyrants we hate?
At their word must I toil at the loom,
And on costliest tissues rich-dyed
The great deeds of Athené illume,

When she smote down our country's pride.

Or harness, with silks many-blended,
Of crimson and saffron hues bright,
The steeds of her chariot made splendid
In the sheen of a silver light?
Or 'broider the rage of the Titans
On the hem of her peplum of gold,
As they waged 'gainst the proud son of Chronos
The war of the giants of old?

Antistrophe

'Mid the grief and the tears
Of the slow-rolling years,
With the taunts of the stranger
Still vexing our ears;
When the music grows faint
That we heard in our youth,
And the heart's wildest plaint
Wakes no pity or ruth.

No smile then will soothe us
Of kindred or home,

No hand weave a garland
To lay on our tomb;
When each morrow brings sorrow
And shadows of dread
And the rest that seems best
Is the sleep of the dead.

Strophe

Alas, for the fair nurtured daughters
Of Ilion, made desert and drear
By the burnings, the ruins, the slaughters,
Of the death-bearing Argive spear.
Accursed be the victim's elation,
Accursed be the chains of the slave,
And woe to the people and nation
That must choose between bonds or a grave;
Ever cursed be the doom of this hour,
On kindred and country it falls,
And the bride must go forth from her bower
To the gloom of the dread Hades halls.

— *Published in* Kensington: A Monthly Magazine, *April 1880.
Oscar had published his own translation of the same passage from*

Euripides' Hecuba *in the Trinity College Dublin poetry magazine,*
Kottabos, *for Michaelmas Term 1876. His version began:*

O fair wind blowing from the sea!
Who through the dark and mist dost guide
The ships that on the billows ride,
Unto what land, ah, misery!
Shall I be borne, across that stormy wave,
Or to whose house a purchased slave?

Oscar Wilde (of whom you ask for further information) is a recent B.A. from Magdalen, Oxford; he is not a fool, for he took a first in Greats, and many think he carries his eccentricities so far, because they give him a name, and get him an entrée into London society. His photograph is in all the shop-windows — long hair, close-shaved face, loose cravat, & velvet coat, with his hands clasped under one cheek, gazing into vacancy. His 'latest' was to go to a ball with a rose upside-down in his button-hole; this was, of course, remarked on. 'Ah,' said he, 'if I wore it in the vulgar fashion, it would look as if I had bought it with gold; but now! — now it looks as if some fair young creature had offered it me, and abashed at her own boldness, had tucked it hastily in my coat, and fled away' — which is, I think, truly absurd & delicious.

— *William King Richardson to Dudley Lincoln, 17 April 1881*

He once told me that at Oxford he noticed that Phil Burne-Jones always guided him past a certain bookseller's window (Shrimpton's perhaps) till one day he said, 'No, Phil! We will see what there is in this window,' and there, to his high enjoyment, among other caricatures, was one of himself by Phil himself.

— Otho Lloyd to A.J.A. Symons, 22 May 1937

On the same occasion the merits of Irving – then attracting the town – came up for discussion. Wilde was a warm supporter of the actor's methods, and indulged in a strain of exaggerated praise over the performance then holding the boards at the Lyceum. 'But what about his legs?' inquired an irreverent listener. 'Irving's legs,' answered Wilde, with the manner of a man who is promulgating some eternal truth – 'Irving's legs are distinctly precious, but his left leg is a poem!'

— *William Mackay*, Bohemian Days in Fleet Street (*1913*)

Reminds me of a good tale of Oscar, when the ticket collector would not let him pass the barrier *senza* ticket – in spite of his imposing appearance, and he protesting that it was really ridiculous – the collector extended his arms to press the poet back. Restrained but not subdued, Oscar exclaimed, 'Oh dear. What dreadful hands!'

— *Rennell Rodd to [unknown], 15 August 1882*

Oscar Wilde, paying a morning visit to a lady, surprised her dusting some articles of *vertù* too precious to be entrusted to any hands but her own. 'Oh!' said he, 'What unnecessary labour! Dust should never be removed. It is the bloom of time.'

— *'Varieties'*, Leicester Chronicle and Leicestershire Mercury,

25 March 1882

Ah! that airy young gentleman is a *poseur*, there's no mistake about that, but he's a deuced sight cleverer than they think. A fellah doesn't take a double-first at Oxford for nothing; beside, he has written some noble lines. Then he knows a lot about art and nearly everything about painting. I saw him, one morning at the Academy, spot, with unerring accuracy, every picture worth looking at. It's true there were not a great many; but such as they were he spotted 'em.

— *John Coleman*, Charles Reade As I Knew Him (*1903*)

The next night, I met him at tea [at Oxford], and his conversation was great fun . . . He said, 'There is really no objection to be urged vs. the pictures at the Royal Academy except that they are not paintings, and are not art at all.' The amusing thing is that to have a picture hung in the Academy is the highest ambition of almost all English painters.

— *William King Richardson to Dudley Lincoln, 29 May 1881*

Herbert Spencer describes Oscar Wilde as 'that outlandish person who attempted to reconcile idiocy with art, and namby-pambyism with sentiment'.

— Marin County Journal, *5 October 1882*

The great Oscar Wilde was there, who appeared in a brown velvet sack-coat, a waving green-blue cravat, and huge trousers. His clean-shaven face & long hair made him the model of an aesthete, and I was glad to see him. The next night, I met him at tea, and his conversation was great fun. A man came in just from London – 'Hullo, Oscar,' said he, 'I visited your room just before I left London, and your magnolia was in full blossom.' 'Did it have the heart to bloom in my absence; how *sweet* of it!' replied Oscar.

— *William King Richardson to Dudley Lincoln, Balliol,*
29 May 1881

'Oscar Wilde,' she said, 'is constantly with us. In front of our house is an almond-tree. One day last spring when it was in full bloom, he stood at the window gazing at it. I said to him, "Is it not too beautiful?" and he answered: "I should like to be asked to your house simply to meet that almond-tree. I should even prefer it to a tenor voice."'

— Echoes of the 'Eighties: Leaves from the Diary
of a Victorian Lady [*Mrs Humphrey Ward*],
ed. *Wilfred George Partington, 1921*

On the night of the first production of *Patience* at the Opera Comique, London [21 April 1881], when many of the celebrities of Society, and Literature and Art were gathered to witness and enjoy the clever *caricature* of the aesthetic, which rumour had promised them, the cynosure of all eyes was one tall, beardless, pale-faced, long-haired self-contained young man. When he entered the theatre with measured and majestic tread, a storm of ironical cheers greeted him, for every one present knew that he was Oscar Wilde, the apostle and bard of the 'Aesthetic'. It was a curious spectacle to see in the stalls in front, the *original*, and on the stage before his eyes, imitating his attitudes, motions and enunciations, the *caricature*. Mr Wilde's observation was: 'If these men [meaning Du Maurier, the artist of *Punch*, and Grossmith who was 'Bunthorne' in the cast at the Opera Comique] choose to caricature me for gold, they can do so.'

— Newspaper cutting, 21 October [1881],
in Colonel Morse's scrapbook

When I met him in a London drawing-room he came up and talked to me in his most affected style; but I soon showed him I did not care for either symphonies or neurotics, and when I mentioned casually he was casting pearls before swine and wasting jewels many others would be glad of, he gave a good humoured laugh and talked delightfully until retrieved by his mother . . . .

— [Mrs] *J.E. Panton*, Leaves from a Life (*1908*)

Blanche Roosevelt, the former opera-singer turned occasional journalist, was asked, after a meeting in London, how Oscar Wilde had struck her:

He struck me as being very, very 'utter'. He was dressed in light pantaloons and a grey redingote buttoned so tightly that it displayed a profusion of wrinkles. He looked as if he had hard work to get into it. He is a large-sized man, with enormous feet and hands, and makes a conspicuous feature in every throng, but his face has a decidedly animal-like expression . . . offset by the originality of his conversation, in which, being a poet, he occasionally utters bright things . . . He told me he thought of coming to America to see what we are like, and referred with apparent pleasure to the flattering manner in which some of his poems had been received by a portion of the American press.

— *The* New York Tribune *quoted in the* Memphis Daily Appeal,
14 October 1881

I was sitting at Romano's in the company of that clever and ill-fated genius shortly after the trial of Lefroy [late 1881]. Wilde was amusing the company with his affectations and paradoxes. 'If,' he said, in his ineffably superior way –'If I were not a poet, and could not be an artist, I should wish to be a murderer.' 'What!' exclaimed one of us, 'and have your portrait-sketch in the *Daily Telegraph*?' 'Better that,' cooed Wilde, 'than go down to the sunless grave unknown.'

— *William Mackay*, Bohemian Days in Fleet Street

(*London*, 1913)

To Oscar Wilde

Your volume like a Provence lute antique
Blent with a classic lyre, were fitlier wrought.
So richly apposite its theme and thought,
Its art so Gothic yet its aim so Greek!

Till now we had dreamed that one alone might seek
From poetry what you with victory sought:
To blend those pure strains the Sicilian taught
With Spenser's line, luxurious and unique!

Nay, since your reverenced Master dwells afar,
It has been given your spirit, I am sure,
To pass, deep-trancèd by slumber's opiate sweets,
High up some white stair sheer to some white star,
And meet, in its immortal vestiture,
The splendor that men mean when they name Keats!

— *Poem by Edgar Fawcett, on receiving, from the author, a copy
of* Poems; *published in the* Literary World, *a Boston periodical,*
29 July 1882

Oscar was neither the only — nor the first — member of the Wilde family to write about Salome and her alluring dance. His older brother Willie contributed the following sonnet to the Trinity College Dublin poetry magazine, Kottabos, *for Michaelmas term 1878:*

Salome
(For a Picture)

The sight of me was as devouring flame
Burning their hearts with fire, so wantonly
That night I danced for all his men to see!
Fearless and reckless; for all maiden shame
Strange passion-poisons throbbing overcame
As every eye was riveted on me,
And every soul was mine, mine utterly —
And thrice each throat cried out aloud my name!

'Ask what thou wilt,' black-bearded Herod said.
God wot a weird thing do I crave for prize:
'Give me, I pray thee, presently the head
Of John the Baptist.' 'Twixt my hands it lies.
'Ah, mother! see! the lips, the half-closed eyes —
Dost think he hates us still now he is dead?'

Though not yet thirty, he has taken warning by the follies of his sire, and is reasonably correct, which so surprised the aristocracy that they are lost in admiration at his exceptionally virtuous example.

— *'Who is Oscar Wilde?'*, Sacramento Daily Record Union
(California), *10 September 1881*

My Dear Sir:

Replying to your questions, I would say that the pure man, like the lily, is unsullied by the mire in which he may grow. The blossom of the tree never looks to the soil about its roots, but is sustained by the trunk and the branch until it has offered up its incense, diffused abroad its fragrance, and accomplished its work. The perfect fruit is garnered by the husband-man; the other falls to decay and dust. This is the divine order for development: first, the germ of life, then the leaf, and then the ripened ear. First, the vegetable, the animal, and then the spiritual man, born of the Spirit, of the Lord of heaven, and not to be again brought into bondage to his own desires. Man's first duty is to bring himself into subjection to the King, and swear eternal fealty unto Him, winning others by His law of love, never coercing to govern them by the word. Caesar, Brutus, and Nero used coercion, and their kingdom is always divided, but the kingdom of God is all in all, and the Prince of Peace is on the throne. His kingdom is one.

I am most respectfully, your obedient servant,

Oscar Wilde.

— 'Oscar Wilde' to the editor of the Chicago Inter-Ocean Times, 27 September 1882. The letter would seem to be one of several forgeries — or inventions - that appeared in the American press during 1882, purporting to have been written by Wilde.

Oscar Wilde: 'A man of true greatness creates one original thing, and only one, during his life.'

— Salt Lake Herald (*Utah*), 2 October 1881

The sky is panther-spotted and the moon
Sleeps like a leopard by the dried up stream.

— *Oscar Wilde poetry notebook*

O.W. and I were discussing Tennyson. I granted his flabby wordiness and stilted tricks of language but upheld his morality. He [Wilde] was really indignant and said that, 'No decent man could have written *Merlin & Vivian*. It is worse than Shelley's *Cenci*: a very old man and a young girl.'

— *G.T. Atkinson to A.J.A. Symons, 15 June 1931*

It is not till after dinner that Mr Wilde shows his wonderful power as a *raconteur* and observer of mankind. I noticed that he has a way of avoiding repartee by carrying on his conversation uninterruptedly ... When asked 'Whom do you consider the *greatest living Poet?*' our illustrious guest deprecated so personal a question, but frankly avowed his conviction that his well-known predecessor, W. SHAKESPEARE, was in many respects quite valuable. Questioned as to Contemporary Poets, [Mr Wilde] said 'ALFRED TENNYSON is a prolific, though somewhat old-fashioned writer, whose verses, I am given to understand, have an extensive sale, but who does not appear to advantage in a court suit. SWINBURNE, though in some respects in sympathy with myself, has, I fear, contracted a fatal taint of Bohemianism, perhaps from living in an unaristocratic neighbourhood. BROWNING is a conscientious, though somewhat uneven writer. As to MORRIS, his verses are prosy, but his wall-papers are eloquently poetical.' The Poet spoke in general terms of general approval of Art, the Moon, Wine, and Republicanism, to which latter, it is no secret that he has sought to convert English Royalty.

— *Parody of Wilde's conversation in 'A Poet's Day',*
Punch (*1882*)

To the Poet, Oscar Wilde

White-throated stranger hast thou come to sing
Where ceaseless sounds of tuneless anvils ring?
Come with thy lute and love-lorn madrigal
To woo to dalliance labor's interval?
Alack! Our very bird-pierced skies
Are mute of melodies . . .

— *Anonymous American poet, 1882*

'How many tenses are there?' asked the teacher of a boy.

'Seven,' answered the boy. 'The present, the perfect, the imperfect, the pluperfect, the first future, the second future, and the Oscar Wilde.'

'Why,' asked she, 'what tense is he?'

'Oh,' replied the boy. 'He's in-tense.'

— *Syndicated 'joke' from the* South Australian Weekly Chronicle
(Adelaide), 2 January 1886

Last Thursday I went to a party at Mrs General McClelland [*sic*]. It was very pleasant and in the midst of the evening she tapped me on the back and turning I was introduced by her to Oscar Wilde. I laughed outright for I could not help it. He has a dead white face with small eyes and no eye lashes. His mouth is always open, showing long white front teeth pressing into his under lip and hair parted in the middle and falling straight down lankly below his ears. Then it gets an inward curve & meets under the chin like a horse collar. His coat was cut very short-waisted in front and the tails fell to his heels. He was in knee-breeches and silk stockings and had a 'crushed strawberry' handkerchief thrust in his breast, and talked in a measured, sepulchral tone. I laughed all the time for I found it impossible to do otherwise.

— *Phoebe Pember to Clavius Levy, New York, 16 January 1882*

OSCAR AND WALT. That Yawp.

At last. It is done. They have met—
O. Wilde, the Flower of the Utter, and
W. Whitman, the Boomer of the Boundless.
They have met. They have.
And the earth still swings through the spaces, and at the same
old stand the equator continues in business.
This is the mode of their meeting—the song of their
swigging and sundering.
This is the ode of their greeting— the yowl, the yawp
barbaric—
The strong and stridulous strain of the steam calliope of the
Un-Art—
The orison of the orbs Uncurbed—
The paean of the pork-house whistle,
Pitched in the key of Whitman.
To the racket, totter and tumble;
Lift up your ears and hear it.

'Yes, it is true,' said Walter, or in words to this effect; 'he
    came to see me this evening, here in my eyrie at Camden.
'And I took him in—
In and in: and up; and up to the innermost, uppermost ins
    and ups of my den in the tertiary story.'
(At least, in something after this fashion he would probably
    have expressed his account if he had written instead of
    spoken it to the reporter.)
'There,' he said to a reporter, before they mounted the stair
    steps.
'There is the spot where Wilde and myself absorbed, got
    away with a bottle.'
And the reporter probably was touched to the tough
By the tender bits of fancy,
And, mayhaps, by the testimony of ocular observation that
    nary another bottle was there or forthcoming as a subject
    of absorption.

'Here,' resumed the roarer of the 'Old Rough', 'here is my
    den and here caracoled we, young Oscar and Oi;
Here we were as "thee and thou" each to the other;
Here we are as soul to soul, as poet to poet;
Aye, we were bobbyshalics;

We were the juncture of the Gospel of the Gone and the Cult
of the Coming;

We were the swaling suture, the kissing conflux of the
quintessential extracts of the fourteenth and twenty-fourth
centuries—

You heerd me?

Do you marvel then that here we had a royal octavo gilt-
edged communion;

That we sealed and delivered a pact as pure as filtered blushes
of modest maidens and as firm as the obstinacy of their
paternal progenitors;

That we had an altitudinous ancient time?

Do you catch on? Do you cling? Do you clamp?

One of the first things I said was: "Oscar, I shall call you
Oscar."

And he answered me, he did: "I like that so much."

Yoh! And he inclined to me; he leaned over; he laid his hand
on my knee. (*Tableau.*)

He did. It was lum-th-tum; it was twee-twee; it was um!

And I, me, Walt, the unhide-bound, I up again and said to him:

"Oscar, you must be a-thirst; I will make some punch."

And his repartee clave swift and clean as a cimetar, as a
straw-cutter:

"Yes, I am a-thirst."

Ha, ha! Ho, ho! Hum!

And I brewed him a brew; I milked him a milk; I punched him a punch.

And he tossed it off as quickly as quickness; as quickly as I could erupt a double calendared, chain electrified, polychodecametric couplet to the tufted tawn of Leona's locks.

Or to the gruesome grimness of Destiny's grip. Yi-yi.

And then we confluxed some more.

He told me that he had been fed on Whitmanesque poetry from childhood; that Lady Wilde was wont to administer my rip staves to him with his porridge.

He has grown up to be a splendid fellow; how could he help it? It is strange why people mock and jeer him so.

He gave to me many mouthsome messages, which the lustrouest of Britain's bards had shipped to me; he said of American poets:

"We in England think there are only two—Walt Whitman and Emerson."

He is a splendid fellow. It is strange why people mock and jeer him so.

He is a clever boy; I like him. Once this remark came to me from him like a springbok through the glade, like a cup caudled canine around the corner:

"I remember you have written: 'All beauty comes from
    beautiful blood and a beautiful brain'; and, after all, I think
    so too."
Aye! and he did not insist on adding,
"And from beautiful breeches; black breeches; knee
    breeches."
We spent two hours together; he and I; me and him; yaas,
    too-too hours; whoopee!
And when he left I lifted up my lips;
I lilted to the lilyful in this lingo—to-wit:
"Good-by, Oscar; God bless you."
Yes, I did, though.
I should hump to howl!'

— *A Whitmanesque account of Oscar Wilde's visit to Walt
    Whitman in Camden on 19 January 1882*, Daily Globe
    (Minneapolis), 29 January 1882

Well, you seem to be having amazing fun over there. We all feel a little jealous. And then your statements are amazing of course, but you must not assert yourself so pointedly when you come back, you see you've no one to contradict you! – Which is bad for you! We were surprised to read, that Mr Wilde declined to eat, on hearing the ladies were upstairs. It was never so known in Israel.

— *Rennell Rodd to Oscar Wilde, 1882*

But what will you say when I tell you that when the door opened I *actually had the pleasure* (?) of punching O.W. in the back with my umbrella – as we rushed for seats – *And* when we got in the Pullman my number was 5 and his 6 – Well I gazed upon the 'soulful eyed' for some time, and at last as he looked up from his paper ventured to ask him how he liked our magazines – and after that for more than half an hour I never heard a man talk as he did – There is no doubt of the fascination of his conversation – for unless he tells everyone the same things he told me it was simply wonderful, especially his descriptions of Whistler's paintings – He merely informed me that *he* made Whistler's reputation – though in my humble estimation Whistler did his best work before Oscar had left Mamma Wilde's apron strings.

— *Joseph Pennell to Elizabeth Robins Pennell,*
19 January 1882

The American people are nothing if not practical. The question ever on their lips is *cui bono?* They care little for the abstract, the rhetorical, the remote. But they are extremely ready to recognize and applaud the immediate, the practically useful. They ardently want instruction and cheerfully receive it.

As a rule the education of audiences is superficial and their opportunities of art culture have been scanty. This must be taken into account. Our people are also impatient to apply what they learn. Whatever art-theory is laid down should be copiously illustrated by applications to daily life. This would teach them its meaning without effort.

For these reasons a series of serial articles on the points of art closest to everyday life would be most welcome to readers. The three topics suggested are the house, the clothing, and the rules for selecting the good from the bad, the true from the false, in buying works of art, especially pictures.

The scheme I append indicates this more in detail. I would like you to elaborate it into three articles of about 1,000 or 1,200 words each. I shall be pleased to pay you $100 for each article. Could I ask that you send me the first article in a week from [this] date?

Theme: Modern Estheticism Applied to Real Life

1. The Home. Its building (architecture). Its furnishing (decoration). Canons of art to be observed.

2. The costume. Its paintability. True principles of fashion. Colours & Cuts. Defence of individuality in attire.

3. Recognition of Merit in Art Products: What makes a masterpiece? Essential relations of the different elements of painting. True and false methods of work in art.

— *Robert S. Davis* [*editor of* Our Continent] *to Oscar Wilde,*
20 January 1882

There were plenty of sunflowers and ox-eyed daisies in the room, and although they were artificial they were very faint indeed. A group of young girls went up together to be introduced [to Oscar Wilde] and little Miss Nordhoff, who is bright enough to do anything, affected naïveté.

'Oh do talk to me a little,' said she.

'I would gladly talk to you the whole evening,' replied my lord.

'Oh pray, tell me,' she rejoined with the deliberate intention that he should make himself ridiculous. 'Pray tell me, Mr Wilde, were you *born* great?'

He was equal to the occasion. I have no doubt that he will go to his grave thinking that Miss N believes him to be a great man, but he looked at her as insolently as he looked at me, a woman old enough to be his mother, and announced, 'Little girl, you had better go and get some ice cream.'

— *Caroline Healey Dall, diary (Massachusetts Historical Society),*
21 January 1882, on encountering Wilde at a meeting of the
Georgetown Literary Club, chez Mrs Hodgson Burnett

Great movements must originate with the workmen. I believe in practical art. I believe the musical value of a word is greater than its intellectual value and nowhere is this better exemplified than in that supreme imaginative work of the young American [Poe] who wrote 'The Raven'. To educate and refine a country you must begin with the masses. There must be stately and simple architecture in your cities and bright and simple dress for men and women. You should have among your people some permanent canon and standard of taste. Creeds and philosophies decay, but beauty is the only thing time cannot harm. We should have in our houses things that gave pleasure to the men who made them.

— *'Wilde in Utica: Ye Last Sweet thing in Oscars'*,
Utica Daily Observer, *7 February 1882*

Oscar Wilde's 'Private Expenses'

Feb 23 Cincinnati

Receipts: $564.00
Lecture: ['Decorative Art']
Private Cash/Drafts:
Private: $74.87 [see below]
Personal: $24.25
Business: $21.67
Total: $120.79

Laundry $5.92 Wine $7 Flowers $3 Messenger $1.75

$17.67

Clark $4.65 Carriages $25 Papers $0.90 Extra Meal $1

$31.55

Wine $3 Papers & Postage $3.25 2 pr Hose $11

$17.25

3 pr Gloves $5.70 Trunk $0.75 Stephen $1.35 Mess $0.60

$8.40

_____

$74.87

Of the 140 lectures that Wilde delivered in North America during 1882, the highest grossing was the first (at New York's Chickering Hall), which took $1,211.00, although the lectures in Philadelphia, Boston and Chicago grossed almost as much. The lowest return was at Aurora, Illinois, on 3 March, where the receipts were just $7.35 (against total expenses of $15.32).

The 'Stephen' listed in Wilde's 'Private Expenses' was probably his black valet, Stephen Davenport. Davenport's wages were paid for by the Carte Company, the promoters of Wilde's tour, so this seems to have been an additional remuneration.

The good in art is not what we directly learn from it but what we indirectly become through it. All the arts are fine arts and all the arts are decorative arts. By separating the handicraftsman from the artist you ruin both.

— *'Wilde in Utica: Ye Last Sweet thing in Oscars'*,
Utica Daily Observer, *7 February 1882*

the sun reels like a drunken Bacchanal into the purple winevat of the west.

— *MS note for a poem*

Coates House
Kansas City
17 April 1882

Dear Sir –

I regret so much that I was not fortunate enough to find you at home, and thank you in person for the beautiful poem you have addressed to me, a poem as swift and as strong and as simple as the sea is. The fourth and sixth verses delight me particularly, but indeed, about the whole poem there is a magic and mystery, and a splendour of spirit that soars high though never out of sight and catches on iridescent wings the glory and gladness of all beautiful things.

I should be sorry to leave Kansas City without seeing you; after my lecture tonight at the hall if you will come round I would be so pleased.

In any case, believe me,
Most truly yours

Oscar Wilde

— Oscar Wilde to George W. Warder ('the bard of Kansas City'),
Sedalia Weekly Bazoo, *5 September 1882. This letter seems
more convincing than others reproduced in the press during Wilde's
American sojourn, and is probably genuine. Warder had published a
long poem, 'A Greeting to Oscar Wilde' in the* Kansas City Times,
*which included the couplet: 'O! the beautiful in beauty! O! the
loveliness in love! | O! the sweetness of suggestion in fair
Venus and her dove . . .'*

He [the average American] is the most splendid egoist, and frequently demonstrates qualities as the most magnificent liar the world produces. He regards the size of his country as a personal compliment of nature to himself.

— *'Oscar Wilde At Home'*, Philadelphia Times,
28 January 1883

I rarely can stay in any city long, but am become a sort of civilized vagrant, an artistic tramp, wandering over the wide unfinished world, my only reward being that I have learned the minor virtues, such as punctuality and getting up early; but they after all are unattractive.

— *Oscar Wilde to Mrs Botta, 11 May 1882*

My dear Mr Wilde,

I received your picture and thank you very much for remembering me. I think it a perfect likeness. Since you were here I (and some boys in the Yard) had a circus. It was very nice. I wish you could have been here. Our dog (a Golden Setter), my goat, and my sister's kittens all performed, and we sold lemonade, and one boy, Ned Higbee, beat the drum. It was awful jolly. If you will come here again, I will take you fishing, and to the top of Bunker Hill monument, and I will repeat something better to you than '[The Ride of] Jennie McNeil', and besides, I will get up another circus. Last night we went to see *Patience*, but we did not like it much. It was the Boston Ideal Company (Miniature). Papa thought my circus was the best. Mother & Father join me in kind regards. And do not forget your little friend,

Porter Chandler.

— *Porter Chandler, the thirteen-year-old son of Rear-Admiral Ralph Chandler, based at the Boston Navy Yard.*

He-ah in California you have be-utiful marbles, but what do you do with them? Do you, like ancient Greek and Roman Republics, fashion them into be-utiful forms? I fear not. I fear that you u-su-al-ly convert them into steps for your dwelling houses.

— *Parody of Oscar Wilde's delivery*, Alta California,
6 April 1882

30% chose to attend because they were determined NOT to be convinced by O.W.'s 'tomfoolery' and wanted to experience his 'bunk' at first hand.

13% came because their 'wives insisted'.

10% were open minded, and wanted to hear what O.W. had to say.

10% various other reasons.

9% 'wanted to see and hear the Dam-phool on general principles'.

1% admitted to being 'honest admirers of Oscar'.

— *A breakdown on audience motives for attending Oscar Wilde's lecture at Platt's Hall, San Francisco,* Daily Report (*San Francisco*), *28 March 1882*

Mr Wilde – says one [American] journal – appeared the other evening at Delmonico's apparelled in a brownish-yellow suit of corduroys . . . Corduroy used to be regarded in some parts of England as a punishment by severe parents upon children too careless of their dress.

— *'Notes on News'*, Wrexham Advertiser, *22 July 1882*

7 August: Narragansett Pier, [$] 100

9 August: Ballston, 22

10 August: Saratoga, 300.47

11 August: Sharon Springs, 84.38

12 August: Cooperstown, 63.94

14 August: Richfield Springs, 137.60

15 August: Kaatirskul, [*figure missing*]

18 August: Tremper House, 61.89

19 August: Strand Hotel, 62.13

21 August: Seabright, 113.04

22 August: Long Branch, 217.10

23 August: Spring Lake, 172.00

24 August: Asbury Park, 168.80

26 August: Cape May, 144.62

Total Receipts [$] 1,760.57

Expenses: 658.81

Net Profit: 1,101.76

60% 661.05

40% 440.71

Mr Wilde's a/c

By 60% as above 661.05

To Private Expenses: 37.09

Balance due: 623.96

Settled in full as above, 2 September 1882, [*signed*] Oscar Wilde

— '*Receipts from lectures, US Summer Tour*'

'There is nothing new in America – except the language.'

— *A. Edward Newton*, Oscar Wilde (*1912*)

My dear Steele,

I have spoken to the Griffin and to the lovely creature he guards – and told them you *might be induced* to accept the superintendence and management of the production of my tragedy – the *Duchess of Padua*. I explained to them that you must have absolute control of everything and everybody.

They agreed.

Now she wants this produced by January 22nd, and I think we might bring this out first – as it affords a real opportunity for artistic setting and mounting which the Nihilist Drama [*Vera*] does not. They or rather *she* is ready to spend *any money on it*. She is dreadfully alarmed at the prospect of its non-production – and I told her it could not be produced unless a great deal of money was spent on it.

Now I want you to write and make an appointment with her at Fifth Avenue Hotel this week. *He* is a brute – a γρυφον [gryfon]– a padded horror – with none of the showman's idea – but she is simple and good, and tractable and lovable – and with you as the practical manager success will be assured. After this we will do the *Nihilists* – and *then the world is at our feet!*

But to begin with the *Nihilists* would be very foolish; as it affords no opportunity for artistic and beautiful setting. It is a play 'Charlie Harris' could almost mount!

I lecture in Pawtucket, Friday, North Attleboro, Saturday. Will be at Boston Sunday (Hotel Vendome) –

O.W.

— *Oscar Wilde to Steele MacKaye* (*in Percy MacKaye*, Epoch: the Life of Steele MacKaye, Genius of the Theatre, in Relation to His Times & Contemporaries (*1927*)

'England,' Wilde said, 'is a garden – England is a growth. Boston is an invention.'

'And New York?' I asked.

'New York is a piece of "dry goods" on a counter.'

— *Elizabeth Robins*, Both Sides of the Curtain (*1940*)

He smoked cigarettes constantly, but apparently did not inhale the smoke, as habitual cigarette smokers do.

— Wheeling Daily Intelligencer (*West Virginia*),

14 August 1883

Epigrams

Il me faut des lions dans des cages dorées: c'est affreux, après la chair humaine les lions aiment l'or, et on ne le leur donne jamais.

Interruptions have not merely their artistic value in giving the impression that the dialogue is created by the actors and not by the author, but they have their physical value also: they give to the actor time to breathe, and fill his lungs again.

Nothing is worth painting except what is not worth looking at.

The Greeks discovered that 'le beau était beau': we that 'le laid est beau aussi'.

Ready-made beauty – for the bourgeois.

— Paris notebook, 1883

My dear Mr Wilde,

Will you come to my studio tomorrow afternoon or Thursday morning. You will find me still working on my portrait of Mrs Gautreau which will go to the Salon on Thursday if it is finished and good. They will tell you I'm out but you must come and knock at the door toc toc toc. You will see my sitter who looks like Phryne.

— *John Singer Sargent to Oscar Wilde* (*1883*)

The education of women is *the* question that concerns our day. The lecture [in Dublin, on 'the higher education of women'] was exhilarating though not very thorough, and afterwards people got up and spoke. But the only speech which was worth anything, was from young Oscar Wilde. He looks 'wild' with a magnificent face, drooping shoulders and a head like a Highland stag; but all my goodwill towards him was completely killed when I saw that he wore white kid gloves and never took them off. I don't know him but he drinks.

— *Alice Maud Meredith, 'Diary', January 1879*

Oscar always said that women would be wonderful if they had not been taught to speak.

— Self-Portrait: Taken from the Letters & Journals of Charles Ricketts, R.A., *collected and compiled by T. Sturge Moore (1939)*

'I like to detect intelligence in men. I do not like to find it in women. Their mission in life is to be beautiful – that is all!' Beautiful women, in Wilde's mind, ought to have the same privilege that men of genius would possess in the ideal world he describes – that is to say, there should be no restraint put upon them. No laws of country, conventions of society, or prejudices of class should hamper them.

— *F.E. McKay, 'A Clever Dramatist's Eccentric Views',*
Kate Field's Washington, *4 April 1894*

The Higher Education of Woman! How absurd; schools and colleges have always seen to the Lower Education of Men. What absurdity is to be completed by the Higher Education of Women. Reverse the process & all will go well. Give women a careful schooling in the arts of sensuality & rational exercise, and a course of learning in the use of the emotions, and there would be no more unhappy marriages.

— *Frank Harris, notes on a dinner with Oscar Wilde at Café Durand in 1899, written in the back of his copy (inscribed by Oscar Wilde) of* An Ideal Husband

When I asked her [Agnes Hughes] about the later tragedy, all she would say was that when he [Oscar Wilde] told her he was going to be married, and to whom, he added — and not as a joke — 'She has only one fault I think: she loves me.'

— *C. Hale-White, 'A Tribute to Mark Rutherford'*
(unpublished memoir)

[I have had a letter from Lord Napier] in which he says, 'Mr Oscar Wilde has laid the basis of a House Beautiful by taking a beautiful wife – the most important piece of living furniture.' Now is not that too good to be kept to myself?'

— *Mary Napier [neé Lloyd] to Oscar Wilde, 24 February 1885*

Oscar Wilde's House

The House – 16 Tite Street, in the same street with Whistler's 'White House', but further from the Embankment, and on the other side of the street. A narrow five-storeyed house (with basement). Decorated under *Godwin*, the well-known architect's guidance (not Whistler, as wrongly stated by Sherard), white-painted front door, with brass knocker (cuivre marteau) and letter-box flap, and windows of frosted glass.

Hall (Vestibule) – Narrow and short, with orange walls up to narrow cream moulding (en teintes dégradantes) and blue frieze above. Small hanging lamp of beaten iron from ceiling, two large white-framed engravings on wall of 'Apollo and the Muses' and 'Diana and Nymphs bathing'.

Library (afterwards the study) on right.

Dining-room (the door facing the front door) – Woodwork in white, and walls in ivory white. All along left-hand wall a hanging cupboard with glass doors, containing specimens of Venetian glass. Two windows (overlooking) small garden, draped with long cream-white curtains of African muslin. Oblong table with table-cloth of unbleached linen – (toile ecru). Old Chippendale chairs painted white to match the room, a silver lamp from Benson's depending from the ceiling, a small green bronze figure of Narcissus on the mantelshelf, a green-blue Morris carpet with white pattern covering the floor.

Staircase (between dining-room and library) – Woodwork white, round brass ball on the enamel stairs covered with golden yellow matting.

Landing on first floor – Dividing front and back drawing-rooms with small white-painted bookcase.

Front drawing-room – Heavy brocaded curtains of dark material (instead of door) at doorway, matted floor, oblong room with bay-window. *Walls* painted a dull green to halfway up then a heavy white painted moulding about a foot broad; above this to ceiling a dull gold Japanese leather paper. Ceiling panelled into squares, inset with old Japanese leather with dragon pattern. From the mouldings of ceiling at four points depended large blue and white barrel-shaped Japanese paper lanterns. *Fireplace* of Queen Anne character, lined with white lilas ([t]iles) and with an iron basket grate. Set into the moulding over the mantelpiece a bronze painted plaque by Donoghue, the American sculptor, of a seated female half-figure, intended as a portrait of Wilde's sister, who died young with the inscription:

Lily like, white as snow,
She hardly knew
She was a woman, so
Sweetly she grew.

On the mantelshelf stood a small marble bust of August Caesar. Right and left of the fireplace fillet the corners were large box-seats heavily cushioned. (Later the right hand seat was removed and a Georgian sofa, covered in green, was introduced.)

Bay-window – Draped with white silk embroidered Syrian curtains.

Furniture – Two cane-seated arm chairs and two simple cane-seated chairs (too slight and slender for Oscar's weight), white-enamelled, designed specially by Godwin, of mixed Greek and Japanese design, an octagon table to match with spindle legs, a small oblong green matted (so-called Japanese) bamboo table (used as a tea-table).

Against the wall a little Louis Seize side-table on which were placed some small 'curios', Japanese, etc., including a gold key said to have been Marie Antoinette's and to have been the key of the Trianon.

Standing against the right-hand wall was a large full-length portrait of Oscar Wilde, in frock coat with the hair curled and holding a cane, said [correctly] by Sherard to have been by [H]arper Pennington but, to my recollection, by Walter Sichert [sic], James Whistler's only pupil.

Against wall between doorway and a curio table was an old settee in gold lacquer and colours (a present from Mrs. Bloomfield Moore).

The cushions in the room were from Liberty and were of a very quiet green with a quite unobtrusive pattern.

Later on, to give more colour, pink satin cushions were brought in.

Hung on the green walls were small white framed lithographs, presents from Whistler, also from Mortimer Menpes (godfather to his younger boy Vyvian), a drawing by Aubrey Beardsley. The manuscript of a sonnet by Keats (given by his sister [in fact, niece] to O.W. in America) and red crayon sketches of relatives and friends of Mrs Wilde.

Back drawing-room – This was a small room, matted like the others and with Oriental rugs spread about. Curtained doorway. Against the right-hand wall was a low wooden platform, cushioned to form a divan. At the windows was lattice-work from Cairo. Just inside the door was a square pillar of wood painted white, into which were set on four sides square plaques of Italian marble, the gift of a friend. Over the doorway and along that side of the room ran a heavy beam and an architrave bearing an inscription from Shelley [in fact, Oscar Wilde], done in gilt and red and blue.

Spirit of Beauty! Tarry still awhile,
They are not dead, thine ancient votaries,
Some few there are to whom thy radiant smile
Is better than a thousand victories.

Later, as the two boys grew and needed more room, this room was turned into Oscar's bedroom . . .

— 'Stray Recollections' by 'Wilde's brother-in-law'
[Otho Lloyd], in The Soil, vol. 1, no. 4 (1914)

Pleasures may turn a heart to stone, riches may make it callous, but sorrows cannot break it. Hearts live by being wounded. Oscar for Constance.

— *MS note on single sheet of paper at BL*

'I am a socialist. Have you been taught to dread them?'

— *Violet Hunt, 'My Oscar' (unpublished memoir)*

Please send Mr Morris's tract on 'Socialism in Art' to Mr Oscar Wilde, 16 Tite St. Chelsea; also 'Commonweal' [*The Official Organ of the Socialist League*'] for the year, beginning with the November number. – 1/9 enclosed & 1d stamp for postage of tract.

— *Jane Morris to Henry Sparling, Autumn 1885*

On another occasion he defended Socialism (of which he knew nothing) against my attacks on the vague ground that it was so 'beautiful' to do as one likes.

— *Walter Sichel*, The Sands of Time (*1923*)

'In each century only three or four men should rule – men of genius – and those men should be allowed to do exactly as they please.' 'Why?' 'Because they have genius. That is superior to anything human. It is a subtle something that is a spark of divinity. It should excuse vagaries, faults, weaknesses, even crimes.'

— *F.E. McKay, 'A Clever Dramatist's Eccentric Views',*
Kate Field's Washington, *4 April 1894*

A lecture on art from one so distinguished and so eccentric as Mr Oscar Wilde is worth hearing. And above all he is a candid critic. 'Your decorations [at the offices of the *Pall Mall Gazette*],' he said, 'are absurd. There is no system obeyed. One thought, like harmony in music, should pervade the whole. Does it? No. They show no soul. Can you exist without a soul? No soul, no harmony, and no –' 'Sunflowers?' suggested someone. 'No. A flower is but an incident.' In critical vein Mr Wilde shook his shorn and curling locks, and, fanning himself with an expansive sage-green silk pocket-handkerchief, proceeded to descant on the maps which hung round the walls. 'A map should be a work of art, with azure oceans limned on its surface, laden with golden galleys, with poops of beaten gold and purple sails. Let each continent show its rugged mountains, its stretching plains. Look at those seething seas of green-hued calico, seas of erysipelas, with big blobs for mainlands and small blobs for islands.' And thus was abuse showered upon those offending sheets. Mr Wilde waved his hand with an attitude of despair, and brushing off a fly from his forehead with the sage-green pocket-handkerchief, he lowered his slim form gracefully into the bosom of a yielding couch.

— Pall Mall Gazette, *24 May, 1884*

Art is not something you can take or leave. It is a necessity of
human life.

— *Oscar Wilde, lecture, 'The Decorative Arts', 1882*

The object of art is to stir the most divine and remote of the chords which make music in our soul; and colour is, indeed, of itself a mystical presence on things, and tone a kind of sentinel.

— *Oscar Wilde, 'Lecture to Art Students at the Royal Academy', 1883*

I send you a programme of the Owl Club which has just been started behind what used to be the York [off St James's]. Oscar Wilde is on the Committee & some of the Rooms are too beautifully done up. His taste when he has been consulted is excellent. We had all sorts of songs & people. A conjurer who was very good, & Harry Conway, etc. A very Bohemian crew but vastly amusing after supper.

— *Adrian Hope to Laura Troubridge, 13 April 1888*

An idea of the Owl Club's Wildean décor is given by an article in the York Herald, *4 February 1888:*

The first thing you see on crossing the threshold is a huge tree, or rather the trunk of a monarch of the forest, on whose leafless branches are perched the night birds in every variety of attitudes. On the walls are old flags, banners, armour of all kinds, imitation tapestry, and pictures, producing a delightful effect. In some rooms there are Japanese decorations, the ceilings are beautifully adorned, and over the whole club there is an air of refinement and luxury.

Oscar's brother, Willie, also contributed to the establishment, composing the Club's motto (after an all-night drinking session):

We fly by night, and this resolve we make:
If the dawn must break, let the d——d thing break.

— *Luther Munday,* A Chronicle of Friendships (*1912*)

'You have come just in time,' said a lady recently to Oscar Wilde, 'and can arrange my screens for me.' Whereupon Mr Wilde replied, 'Oh, don't arrange them – let them occur.'

— Pall Mall Gazette, *22 February 1889*

Meeting Wilde casually at Gatti's where [John] Barlas and I were lunching, Barlas and Wilde were discussing what they should do after lunch. Being near old St James's Hall, I suggested that we go and hear the Wagner matinée announced for that afternoon. And Oscar said: 'Oh no! Music! Oh, my dear fellow, no, no! Music is so violent!'

— *Frank Liebich*, *'Oscar Wilde'* (*unpublished memoir*)

I once met him [Oscar Wilde] at a friend's house and had some talk with him; his opinion that 'after the infinite modulations of the violin, the human voice always strikes aridly on mine ear', did not impress me as particularly true (he probably attached some meaning to the word 'modulations' which I could not fathom), but when he declared that we ought periodically to change the pictures on our walls as the Japanese do when they hang them on rollers, something like the texts one used to see in railway waiting-rooms, I could not but feel he was right, for it is perfectly true that we cease to see the pictures which are in our sight every day, or at least to take rational pleasure in them.

— *J.A. Fuller-Maitland*, A Door-Keeper of Music (*1929*)

Mr Oscar Wilde's reputation would be gone if it became known that he had ever uttered a single speech without a word of nonsense in it. Hence his assertion that 'ugliness was first introduced into art when the first bust or portrait of a man was shown' may be regarded simply as a saving clause, a sort of trademark, like the clown's 'Here we are again!' Otherwise his little speech at the Westminster Town Hall last night [16 October 1885] was full of good sense. His vindication of the aspects of beauty in commonplace city life – even in a hoarding of picture posters – came in aptly, though to most people it is something of a truism. More novel though not less true is his protest against the growing practice of building houses higher than the street they are in is wide. 'Northumberland Avenue,' he said, 'was being rapidly destroyed, the abnormal height robbing the architecture of the play of sunlight, which was one of the chief beauties of any fine building.'

— Pall Mall Gazette, *17 October 1885*

When his friends were looking up train times in Bradshaw, Oscar Wilde said, 'I would sooner lose a train by the A.B.C. than catch it by Bradshaw.'

— *Mrs Claude Beddington,* All That I Have Met (*1929*)

But I had an appreciation for his conversation and for the fact that he devoted half an hour to discussing, among other things specially interesting to me, his impressions of America, '– those stretches of wilderness – the influences, making for culture, of great cities – the townbred man is the civilized being. City life' (I wonder, now, if he didn't say 'town') 'city life nourishes and perfects all the more civilized elements in man. Shakespeare wrote nothing but doggerel lampoon before he came to London, and never penned a line after he left.'

— *Elizabeth Robins*, Both Sides of the Curtain (*1940*)

It was when quoting (or trying to quote) a line from [Wilde's] 'Endymion' that I made the error (unpardonable in Wilde's estimate) of changing a word – and misquoting quite unintentionally. A week later, [John] Davidson told me that whenever my name was mentioned, Wilde had said: 'Liebich! Oh, yes! Liebich is original in all things, including his quotations.'

— *Frank Liebich, 'Oscar Wilde' (unpublished memoir)*

[Epigrams]

Most English artists never paint what they see. They paint what the public sees. And the public never sees anything.

The costume of the nineteenth century is far too sombre. Sin is the only real colour element left in modern life.

People often forget that behind the most commonplace and uninteresting exterior there may be the most commonplace and uninteresting character.

Wickedness is a myth invented by good people to explain the superior attractiveness of others.

It is a great pity that embroidered waistcoats are so little worn nowadays. Waistcoats are one of the few subjects that are really suitable for serious conversation.

Offsets to his brilliant cleverness – He had his days of gloom and depression and reaction when he sulked and brooded and was ineffably bored, and behaved generally like a spoiled child.

— *'Wilde's Personal Appearance'* – *'by his sister-in-law'*
[*Mrs Frank Leslie*], The Soil, *vol. 1, no. 4, 1917*

One of the charming things [said by Wilde] that may fail to get into print is 'Absinthe has no message for me'. He has fearful, vulgar streaks, e.g. he has clippings about himself sent him by the newspaper agency. Poor fellow, he is not so very unlike what I was without thee. He asked me to come to the Café Royal tomorrow. I told him I could not promise. 'Oh, then I shall be alone!' and such a terrible look came into his face, the look of a man who does everything as a *pis aller*.

— *Bernard Berenson to Mary Costelloe, 1892*

Dear Mr Reid,

I write in absolute despair – I find that Wednesday is the birthday of an aunt of my wife's – (a real aunt – that is to say unmarried and with a large income) and we had been engaged to dine with her for the last month – So I must give up my delightful dinner with you – I had quite forgotten when her birthday was, and had only a dim memory of a family party looming in the distance . . .

Yours in humiliation.

— *Oscar Wilde to T. Wemyss Reid, 1887. (Reid was manager of Cassell's, the publishers of* The Woman's World, *the magazine that Wilde edited.)*

I never once saw Oscar enter a pub in England or a bar in Paris. He loved cafés but abhorred saloon bars etc. I have met him sometimes in Fleet Street on his way to La Belle Sauvage Yard [the *Woman's World* offices] and there was never the faintest suggestion of 'going to have a quick one' or anything like that . . . I have never met anyone who saw Oscar drinking in a London bar, or standing up to imbibe.

— *R.H. Sherard to A.J.A. Symons, 13 May 1937*

Oscar Wilde fairly scintillated with wit. The host [T.P. O'Connor] was talking to a radiant blonde, and Oscar Wilde asked Mrs T.P. if she wasn't jealous? She said, 'No – T.P. doesn't know a pretty woman when he sees one.' Harold Frederic said, 'I beg leave to differ – what about yourself?' Mrs T.P. answered, 'Oh, I was an accident.' 'Rather,' said Oscar Wilde, 'a catastrophe!'

— *Mrs T.P. O'Connor*, I Myself (*1910*)

Laugh – Very full and hearty; he would wait to see if you had caught his point, and suddenly burst into a peal of laughter of exquisite enjoyment at his own witticism or joke. His sense of *humour* (as distinct from wit) was great and very infectious, especially in his own home. This side of his nature was not suspected, perhaps, by those who only saw him posing out-of-doors, and he was not given due credit for it.

— *'Wilde's Personal Appearance'* – *'by his sister-in-law'*
[*Mrs Frank Leslie*], The Soil, *vol. 1, no. 4, 1917*

Wilde spoke to me about the necessity of the comic spirit in life.
He said something about it being a purge to all human vanity.

— *Arthur Roberts*, Fifty Years of Spoof, *1927*

[Epigrams]

One should always contradict the aged. One should do it on principle.

The beauty of athletics is a thing that no athletic person knows anything about.

The English are always degrading Truths into Facts. When a Truth becomes a Fact it loses all its intellectual importance.

Thought began with the mystic who gave answers to which there were no questions. It has ended with the man of Science who asks questions to which there are no answers.

The artist can see everything except the obvious.

To look bored is ~~often very~~ becoming. To be bored never is.

Idleness is the condition of perfection.

The worst way in which to begin one's day is by being brilliant at breakfast.

One cannot admire other people too much or other people's work too little.

'To me there are but two terms, civilization and barbarism . . . Conventionalism is the worst form of barbarism. You [Australians] will strike your own keynote, and evolve harmonies in sympathy with your dazzling noon-day. I am a poet of the night – the night of the city and *salon* – luxuriously illuminated, full of passionate sweetness, suffused with the voluptuous colour of perfumes. But for you, I am mute – an Australian Walt Whitman may perhaps lift you to a higher level than mine. At least you will not have to contend against the debasing influence of the Mediaevalists – the influence I am fighting.'

— *'Esmé Colquhoun', a character based closely on Oscar Wilde in Mrs Campbell Praed's* Affinities (*1885*)

'So they are desirous of my beauty at Botany Bay,' said Oscar, inviting my attention to a letter. 'I have inquired concerning this Botany Bay. It is a place of anthropophagi, the abode of lost souls, whither criminals are transported to wear a horrible yellow livery. Even they are called "canaries". So I have written for them a Symphony in Yellow – they will feel the homely touch.'

An omnibus across the bridge
Crawls like a yellow butterfly,
And, here and there, a passer-by
Shows like a little restless midge.

Big barges full of yellow hay
Are moored against the shadowy wharf,
And like a yellow silken scarf,
The thick fog hangs along the quay.

The yellow leaves begin to fade
And flutter from the Temple elms,
And at my feet the pale green Thames
Lies like a rod of rippled jade.

I rhyme 'elms' with 'Thames'. It is a venal offence in comparison with theirs, yet it will show my sympathy. A symphony in sympathy – how sweet! Suppose I were to add a stanza!

And far in the Antipodes
When sobbing suns have sunk to rest
A convict to his yellow breast
Shall hug my yellow melodies.

— 'Oscariana' quoted in The Bookfellow (Australia), 15 November 1914. (Written in response to a request for a poem from the Sydney-based Centennial Magazine in 1889.)

About that time [publication of *The Happy Prince*] he came to stay a few days, between two country-house visits in Dorset, with me and three other friends in a cottage let to us, on Brownsea Island, by our friend Frederick Cavendish Bentinck. As we only had an old woman who came in to cook and 'do' for us there, our ménage was not luxurious, but Wilde seemed thoroughly to enjoy it. His only want was a cup of tea before getting up in the morning, for the getting of which I had to rise, light the kitchen fire, and boil some water. 'My dear Jacomb! I positively cannot open my eyes without a cup of tea.' He joined like a schoolboy in the early-morning plunge in the harbour from the castle steps, and we spent most of our days sailing in small boats in Poole Harbour or on the sea.

— *G.P. Jacomb-Hood*, With Brush and Pencil (*1925*)

I think the heart of every earnest man woman and child (and that means all children) who read 'The Nightingale and the Rose' will cry out a rich thanksgiving of delight to the Author. To me it is nothing less than a miracle to *feel* the gorgeous flood-tide of human passion beneath the surface, and to *see* the delicate and steadfast simplicity of the language. You seem to have engaged with Human Love as the Eye with External Objects. They exist within and without at one and the same time. Speak thus again and again to the Child Nature in these restless days, and quiet the restless adult with reverence for passion. To make even wrongly-directed feeling seem a sacred privilege is to take off the drag from the wheel of Civilization – and to give back to the blue sky its tender interest as the home of the Immortals.

— *Samuel Hales* (*Librarian of the Students' Free Library, Toynbee Hall*) *to Oscar Wilde, thanking him for a copy of* The Happy Prince, *16 June 1888*

Dear Sir,

As the following passages occur in your tale entitled 'The Night-ingale and the Rose' – (1) 'From her nest in the holm-oak tree the Nightingale heard him, and she looked out through the leaves and wondered.' (2) 'But the oak-tree understood, and felt sad, for he was very fond of the little Nightingale, who had built her nest in his branches.' – I take the liberty of writing to you, as I think you may like to know that the Nightingale almost invari-ably builds her nest upon the ground. Books, however, say that it is found occasionally at a level of from one to three feet from the ground; so that, supposing her nest in the holm-oak to be placed as low down as this, it might, strictly speaking, be correct.

Believe me, yours faithfully

J.R. Earle.

— *J.R. Earle to Oscar Wilde, 27 December 1890*

Why, oh! *why* did you not keep to my large margin. I assure you that there are subtle scientific relations between margin and style, and my stories read quite differently in your edition [of *The Happy Prince*].

— *Oscar Wilde to Mr Niles of Roberts Brothers, Boston* (*concerning their printing of* The Happy Prince and Other Tales)

There are but two living writers in this England who observe a true reverence for their immortal language – I am one; you are the other.

— *Stephen Coleridge to Oscar Wilde, 19 March 1890*

[Oscar Wilde:] Fiction – not truth – I could never have any dealings with truth – If truth were to come to me, in my room, he would say to me, 'You are too wilful.' And I should say to him, 'You are too obvious.' And I should throw him out the window.

[Katherine Bradley:] You would say to 'him'? Is not Truth a woman?

[Oscar Wilde:] Then I could not throw her out of the window; I should bow her to the door.

— *'Michael Field', Diary, 21 July 1890*

Willie Maxwell on his love – as a boy – for the 'fairies' that he saw performing at the pantomime in Brighton. Even when he met them off stage – he ignored their commonplace looks and manners – and continued to consider them as 'fairies', and to be spellbound and tongue-tied.

'Later when I spoke of this to Oscar Wilde he said: "But you were quite right, my dear Willie. They *are* fairies. It is only their mothers who are mortal.'

— *W.B. Maxwell,* Time Gathered (*1937*)

Pose – When standing talking – Bent the head forward condescendingly to his listener (a trick inherited from his mother, Lady Wilde) – was easily audible in any drawing-room through the buzz of conversation, and filled and permeated a room with his presence.

Attitude – When *seated and talking* – Leaned forward from his waist towards his listener; fixed his eyes full upon him; made much play with his right arm and hand, moving the arm freely from the shoulder, and letting the large hand with its full and fleshy palm move freely on the wrist.

When he made his point (quand il avait fait son trait) would throw himself back in the chair and look at his auditor as much as to say: 'What can you find to say to that?'

Generally speaking, the effect was that he might have stepped out of the seventeenth century just as he was, into our own times, or from an aristocratic 'salon' of the reign of Louis Quinze.

— *'Wilde's Personal Appearance'* – *'by his sister-in-law'*
[*Mrs Frank Leslie*], The Soil, *vol. 1, no. 4, 1917*

Mrs Wilde had sent me a card for an at-home in their elegant little house in Tite Street, Chelsea. I accepted and found Oscar Wilde posing with his back against the most picturesque piece of furniture in the room. He was dressed in the height of fashion, which included, in those days, lavender-striped trousers, besides a lavender-coloured tie and handkerchief. He was holding a corner of the handkerchief between his teeth and rolling and unrolling it sideways with his fingers, looking regally bored and indifferent. I remember telling [John] Davidson about it later and quoting Oscar's very gracious reception of me – 'Oh, how d'ye do. How kind of you to come and see us' – and Davidson saying, 'Which really meant "What the devil are you doing here?"'

— *Frank Liebich, 'Oscar Wilde' (unpublished memoir)*

Oscar Wilde came to our house [in Grosvenor Place] now and again, but my mother could not bear him, especially his mannerism of standing on the hearth-rug in front of the fire with his back to the company, and there he would pose until he got his huge heavy face in the cheval glass above, directly in line with another cheval glass at the end of the room, and thus he would get rows and rows of himself.

— *Maude Wynne*, An Irishman and his Family:
Lord Morris and Killanin (*1937*)

Wilde has been reproached for his vanity. However, I have seen him as meek as a little child before Walter Pater at a dinner given for us by a friend at the Garrick Club [in 1890]. With a playful deference he called him 'Sir Walter' and he proudly recognized him as his master.

— *Stuart Merrill, 'Oscar Wilde' (unpublished memoir)*

[Epigrams]

One should spend one's days in saying what is incredible, and one's evenings in doing what is improbable.

I can believe anything provided it is quite incredible.

The tragedy of dining out in London is that one always knows what the other people are going to say. The ~~pleasure~~ comedy of dining out in London is that one never knows what one is going to say oneself.

The real object of dining out is to have an opportunity of listening to one's own conversation.

Anything becomes a pleasure if one does it too often.

It is a sad thing that beggars so rarely appeal to one's sense of beauty.

To dine with Oscar Wilde was a privilege that one does not forget. Only those who have known him can ever realize what his personality was: he was a superman.

— *George Ives, Diary, 15 October 1893*

Servants always idolized him, though I have heard one impatiently say that he was too womanish.

— *'Stray Recollections' by 'Wilde's brother-in-law'*
[Otho Lloyd] in The Soil, *vol. 1, no. 4, 1917*

You wisely purpose to add to the story [*The Picture of Dorian Gray*] so as to counteract any damage that may be done by it being always on sale at 1/- as it first appeared in Lippincott. Could you not make Dorian live longer with the face of the picture transformed to himself and depict the misery in which he ends his days by suicide or repents and becomes a better character. Lord Henry too goes off the scene very quickly. Could not he also live a little longer – and you could make an excellent contrast between the death of the two men. This is what has occurred to me. It is for you to decide if it is worth anything.

— *George Lock to Oscar Wilde, 7 July 1890.*
(*Lock was the distributor of* Lippincott's Magazine, *and publisher of the book-version of* The Picture of Dorian Gray.)

If I judged you by what you say in print, I should fear that you were somewhat heartless. Having seen & spoken with you, I conceive that you are just as poor & self-tormenting a creature as any of the rest of us, and that you are simply joking at your own expense.

Don't think me rude in saying that *Dorian Gray* is very very clever. It is more – it is suggestive & stimulating, and has (tho' you may not know it) the anxiety of a human Soul in it. You care far less about Art, or any other word spelt with a capital, than you are willing to admit, and thereby lies your salvation, as you will presently discover.

Though here and there in some pages you parade the magnificence of the Disraeli waistcoat, that article of wardrobe fails to disguise you. One catches you *in puris naturalibus*, and then the Man is worth observing.

— *Robert Buchanan to Oscar Wilde, 5 August 1891*

Mrs Palmer asked at dinner: 'Oscar, what did Dorian do when he went down to Whitechapel?' Oscar Wilde: 'Really, you know, I couldn't possibly tell about that at dinner. If you will come with me, alone, into the conservatory after dinner, I will tell you all about it.'

So, as soon as Mrs Palmer 'gathered up' the ladies in the manner of the day, she and Oscar adjourned to the conservatory. Meanwhile we men, Walter Palmer and two young men from Reading whose names I have forgotten, and I, joined the ladies in the drawing-room. A few minutes later, Mrs Palmer entered almost shrieking with laughter, and motioning to Wilde who had followed her, gasped: 'What do you think this wretch told me? I had asked him to tell me the wickedest thing Dorian Gray did in Whitechapel. And he bent over and whispered into my ear, "He ate peas with a knife."'

— *Frank Liebich, 'Oscar Wilde' (unpublished memoir)*

'The worst of Dickens,' Oscar once said to me, 'is that he is so dreadfully and tediously immoral. He means well, but nothing is more immoral than to mean well – to have a moral intention in a novel. A novel should never have any intention other than to tell a story. Dickens means so well that he must snap the thread of his story to explain what he means, which should never be done.'

'Yes,' I said, 'but in chapter eleven of *Dorian Gray*, which is, otherwise, told always in the third person, you unexpectedly lapse into the first person to say, "I think" this or that which, if done by any other novelist, you would denounce, as inexcusably bad art. A novel should, surely, be told in one person throughout. Moreover, you break the thread of the story, which you have just said should never be broken, by interpolating a lengthy and learned dissertation on musical instruments, precious stones and gems, tapestries, vestments ecclesiastical and otherwise, paintings, and the like, thereby breaking the very rule which you have just laid down.'

But what I had hoped was a 'hit', Wilde parried cleverly by replying evasively:

'Thank you for the graceful compliment you pay me by implying that Dickens was only a novelist, whereas I am an artist; and, for the artist, all laws, whether of art or morals, exist only to be broken at will.'

— *Coulson Kernahan, 'Oscar Wilde: Some Recollections'*
(unpublished memoir)

After dinner that evening Wilde took me into the front room to show me his collection of picture-posters, some laid out on a table, others draped over the backs of chairs, and a few upon the floor. There was not one single poster to which objection could be made on the score of impropriety, but when Mrs Wilde opened the door, and was about to enter, Wilde hastily ushered her out, exclaiming: 'No! No, my dear Constance. These are not for your pure eyes to see.' At the dinner table, that evening, he had remarked that to abstain from doing what one wishes to do, because it is improper, is the sign of arrested intellectual development, and even to his wife, he must needs advertise himself as intellectually superior to other folk by posing as a collector of improper picture-posters – which he was not.

— *Coulson Kernahan, 'Oscar Wilde: Some Recollections'*
(unpublished memoir)

Oscar Wilde disait que nous serions jugés par nos reves.

— *Henri de Regnier,* Les Cahiers inédits 1887–1936

(*2 January 1892*)

Wilde claimed that the change of literary work [from Poetry to Drama] was due to the noise which came from the nursery. 'A dramatic author,' he said, 'can endure tumult, a poet cannot. I – I am a poet no longer.'

— *J.M. Stoddart, prospectus for a proposed US edition of the complete works of Oscar Wilde, c. 1906*

Wilde says he never writes a line in a play or a book without supposing himself the person he makes talk.

— *F.E. McKay, 'A Clever Dramatist's Eccentric Views', in*
Kate Field's Washington, *4 April 1894*

[*Lovel.*] I have written very little since my marriage.

[*Lord Mertoun.*] When a poet has his ideal to pour out tea for him, his inspiration is gone. All great poetry is an aspiration.

[*Lovel.*] I don't think it is that, but all moments for creation come to one suddenly, as a great reaction against one's life.

[He has] a lot of blue china. I hope he lives up to it.

An angel on earth nowadays would have to pay for his wings.

He had given Arthur a terrible black eye, or Arthur had given him [one] – I really don't remember, but I know they were great friends.

He either died of a broken heart or got a situation in the Civil Service. I really am not quite sure which, but I know he was very wretched.

[He has the] philosophy to bear the misfortunes of others.

Women are not made to be believed in or disbelieved in – they're made to be loved.

Those of us live best who crowd into the little span of life the
most fiery-coloured moments.

— *from MS of 'A Wife's Tragedy'*

It was teatime, and a large company was gathered. The duchess took from a vase a magnificent rose in perfect bloom. She inhaled the scent, had it passed round, and everyone went into raptures, for its scent matched its beauty. It came to Oscar – he sniffed it ardently, but then – in a flash – tore off the petals and scattered them on the ground. A tremor of indignation rose against this sacrilege. But Oscar explained – 'It would have been too sad to see such a rose wither.' And the company was duly consoled.

— *René Gimpel, 31 March 1918,* Diary of An Art Dealer *(1963), referring to meeting with Albert Clerk-Jeannotte in 1908*

As long as Oscar Wilde was at Wilton he was the centre of attraction – always talking either to a solitary lady or a group of entranced listeners. Sometimes I thought him amusing, once or twice, brilliant, often fatuous. His great gift is perfect assurance – truly brazen when he is talking nonsense. For when he is quite tired out, he trusts to his deliberate manner of slow enunciation to carry off perfectly commonplace remarks. One evening when he was quite exhausted with successive tête-à-têtes, the smoking-room symposium formed itself as usual with George Wyndham as leader. G.W. really did all the talking, and all O.W. could do was to reiterate very slowly, when reference was made to somebody, or another, 'How old is he?' at which the assembly looked uncommonly interested. He was at his best about art and literature, and thoroughly idiotic about politics and social questions.

— *Charles L. Graves,* Hubert Parry: His Life and Works (*1921*)

His signing of the visitors' book [at Wrest, August 1891] was characteristic. It was a large tome, with large, thick creamy sheets. He did not sign on the same sheet as the rest of the party, but took a fresh sheet, on which he wrote his name towards the top, and then executed an immense flourish, so that no other name could be written on the same page.

— *A.G.G. Liddell*, Notes from the Life of an
Ordinary Mortal (*1911*)

It is the custom, I am told, to consider him completely typical of the end-of-the-century artist – a ridiculously foolish custom. True, he is cynical, *blasé*, rather indolent; but he does not affect the sad satiety of the modern young man, or his hopeless pessimism. Mr. Wilde is determined to take nothing seriously; he will wring a smile from everything. For him life is a brilliant paradox, and death an epigram.

— *'Interesting People'*, Winter's Weekly, *5 March 1892*

[Epigrams]

Credit is the only thing a gentleman should live on.

Those who pay their bills are soon forgotten.

One's button-hole may be allowed to be romantic in feeling, but one's necktie should be distinctly clinical both in style and treatment.

The old should be neither seen nor heard.

To become a work of art is the object of living.

Pleasure is what we take from others, Duty what we expect from others, and Genius what we Deny to others.

One should never be useful. Only the uncivilized are useful.

The smallest affectation will rob virtue of half its goodness.

It is only in the continual contemplation of one's own perfection that one can hope to become perfect.

Wherever the necessities of life are cheaper than the luxuries of life the community becomes uncivilized. Bread should be always dearer than flowers.

When at the end of each year the English make up their national ledger, they balance their stupidity by their wealth, and their vices by their hypocrisy.

There is nothing to be said in favour of anyone's principles. There is much to be said in favour of everyone's prejudices.

In old days men of letters wrote books and the public read them. Nowadays books are written by the public and nobody reads them.

Those who love only once in their lives are the really shallow lovers.

The English are the most extraordinarily hardworking race. They are the only nation now left in Europe that takes the trouble to be hypocritical.

One should never make one's *début* with a scandal. One should reserve that to lend an interest to one's maturer years.

The public are quite charming. The only offensive thing about them is their brass-band. Journalists are the brass-band of the public.

There are as many publics as there are personalities.

A great Empire has been forced on the English. They have carried their burden as far as the Stock Exchange.

Everything is a poison. But there are two kinds of poisons. There are the poisons that kill, and the poisons that keep alive. The last are the more terrible.

Women marry in order to find peace, and take lovers in the hope of having excitement. In both cases they are disappointed.

In old days people had a great respect for grey hair. Now they have a great respect for dyed hair. That shows a distinct advance.

Life is a dream that prevents one from sleeping.

In the development of the intellectual life it is only those who know where they are going that ever lose their way.

The journalist is always reminding the public of the existence of the artist. That is immoral of him.

The journalist is always reminding the artist of the existence of the public. That is indecent of him.

Many movements begin with the appearance of the Disciples, and end with the arrival of the Founder.

Miracles always happen. That is why one cannot believe in them.

The intellectual stagnation of the English as a race is a proof of the fatal influence of a permanent income on thought.

In mad and coloured loves there is much danger. There is the danger of ~~keeping~~ losing them no less than the danger of ~~losing~~ keeping them.

Man can only worship his inferiors. That is the intellectual weakness of all cosmogonies and the emotional strength of all religions.

An artist can create a passion. But no one, except a sentimentalist, can repeat an emotion.

The tragedy of the poor is that they have no real passion for pleasure.

In the presence of a work of art the public should applaud and the journalist be silent.

The applause of the public is the only thing that keeps one from sleeping.

One touch of nature will make the whole world kin. Two touches of nature will ~~destroy~~ ruin any work of art.

The capacity of finding temptations is the test of the culture of one's nature. The capacity of yielding to temptations is the test of the strength of one's character.

Only the weak resist temptation.

To treat the serious things of life very trivially, and the trivial things very seriously, is the only true Philosophy of Life.

Manliness has become quite effeminate. Only women are manly nowadays.

Idleness is a condition of perfection.

Song

A Poet lived in a handsome style,
His books had sold, and he'd made his pile,
His articles, stories and lectures, too,
Had brought success, as everybody knew.
But the Poet was tired of writing tales
Of curious women, and singular males;
So soon as he'd finished his Dorian Gray,
He set to work at a four-act play.

Chorus

A four-act play, a four-act play,
A most aesthetic, very magnetic fancy, let us say;
He'd filled his purse by writing verse, why not a four-act play?
His young disciples expressed surprise,
They said, 'Dear, dear! Do you think it wise?'
The Poet-author made no reply,
Merely winked his left pellucid eye.
The piece came out and it stood the test,
For he'd borrowed only the very best;
And those who came to scoff at the play
Had to hammer applause ere they drove away.

Chorus

They drove away, they drove away,

While this magnetic, peripatetic author remains to say,

He was much delighted that those invited enjoyed his four-act play.

— *From Charles Brookfield*, The Poet and the Puppets, *1892*

Butler. Lord Darlington.

Lady Windermere. How do you do, Lord Darlington. I can't shake hands with you. My hands are all wet with these roses. They came up from Selby today. Aren't they lovely?

Lord D. Ripping.

Lady W. Oh! What dreadful slang you talk. Roses aren't ripping. They are lovely. They are the loveliest things in the world. Oh!

Lord D. What is the matter?

Lady W. One of them has pricked me.

Lord D. How horrid of it to have such sharp thorns. I suppose a rose is the only thing in the world that has ever wounded you.

Lady W. No – you wounded me the other night.

Lord D. I hope you are not serious, Lady Windermere.

Lady W. Oh yes I am.

Lord D. What did I do? Do tell me.

Lady W. Oh, you did nothing wrong. In fact you waltzed charmingly.

Lord D. It is the only serious occupation I have. But you must tell me how I offended you.

— *Early draft of opening scene of* Lady Windermere's Fan

I wish to thank you for a divine pleasure [of seeing *Lady Windermere's Fan*]. No one appears to have had the courage to speak out about your play (except yourself perhaps). We were more than delighted. I think it will outlive the author as the *School for Scandal* has Sheridan. I was much struck with the ease & absence of effort in the flow of its action . . . it will be regarded as a classic.

— *Hermann Vezin to Oscar Wilde, 24 June 1892*

A playwright runs into debt as surely as his play runs into royalties.

— *Coulson Kernahan, 'Oscar Wilde As I Knew Him'*
(unpublished memoir)

[Oscar Wilde said] he would like to protest against the statement that he ever called a spade a spade. The man who did so should be condemned to use one. He had also been accused of lashing vice, but he could assure them that nothing was further from his intentions. Those who had seen *Lady Windermere's Fan* would see that if there was one particular doctrine contained in it, it was one of sheer individualism. It was not for anyone to censure what anyone else did, and everyone should go his own way, to whatever place he chose, in exactly the way that he chose.

— *Oscar Wilde's toast — 'replying for "The Drama"' — at Royal General Theatrical Fund dinner, 26 May 1892, in* Proceedings at the Forty-Seventh Anniversary Festival of the Royal General Theatrical Fund (*1892*)

OSCAR WILDE

'I am not able to write a line,' he said, 'unless I feel inspired. In order to evolve anything I consider worthy of myself, I must feel that I am "possessed" of my subject. I seldom write during the day. It is at night, when all is still, dead almost to the writer, that the mind may soar above earthly considerations. In this I follow the maxims of Gustave Flaubert.'

— *F.E. McKay, 'A Clever Dramatist's Eccentric Views', in* Kate Field's Washington, *4 April 1894*

Mr Kelvil. I consider the House of Commons to be our most admirable institution.

Lord Illingworth. I have nothing to say against the House of Commons. It is the last bulwark of our national stupidity.

Lady Caroline. Do you take no sides in modern politics, Lord Illingworth?

Lord Illingworth. One should never take sides in anything, Lady Caroline. It is most demoralizing. It is the beginning of sincerity. And earnestness follows shortly afterwards. And the human being becomes a bore. As for the two sides in our politics, what are they? A Radical is merely a man who hasn't dined, and a Tory simply a gentleman who has never thought. The underfed argue with the undereducated and the result is modern legislation. However the House of Commons really does very little harm. You can't make people good by Act of Parliament. That is something.

— *MS of 'Mrs Arbuthnot'* – *later* A Woman of No Importance

Mrs Walter Palmer 'animadverted' rather jocosely on Wilde's cheek in telegraphing his acceptance of an invitation, 'if you will give us two rooms, one for Mrs Wilde and one for me'. On the same occasion (at lunch) she told me this: Wilde had lunched tête-à-tête with her the week before and had requested that no servant be present. To this she consented, and had served him, with her own hand, a full-sized slice of cold roast beef, when Wilde asked for some pickles which stood on the side-board. 'And in the two seconds that I turned my back to him to get the pickles, that large slice of beef disappeared. He must have taken it in his fingers,' she added, 'and stuffed it into his mouth!'

— *Frank Liebich, 'Oscar Wilde' (unpublished memoir)*

Wilde's distinctive 'signe' is affirmative hyperbole: 'D'un fait hypothétique, il affirme sa verité, il insiste. Par exemple, il disait à la princesse G: "Il me semble que je vous ai toujours connue. Je veux vous voir tous les jours. Je resterai toujours avec vous; j'ai été toujours avec vous." C'est à ce diner que, s'ennuyant, il disait en sortant: "J'ai voulu me tuer à table, mais les couteaux étaient d'or."'

— *Henri de Regnier*, Les Cahiers inédits 1887–1936, *entry for September 1894*

'I am thinking of publishing a book of maxims called *Oscariana*, which may or may not be acceptable to the thinking world. My idea is that every day should begin with a new thought, a fresh idea, and that "yesterday" should be a thing of the past. Forget everything unpleasant in the past and live for the present and future.'

— *'Oscar Wilde's Philosophy'*, Weekly Standard and Express (*Blackburn*), *16 September 1893*

[Epigrams]

The beautiful mistake of the young is in imagining that Life is a passion, not a philosophy. The horrible mistake of the old is in imagining that Life is a passion, not a philosophy.

Sympathy with suffering is the joy of one leper meeting another leper on the road.

Every now and then England discovers that one of its sores shows through its rags and shrieks for the nonconformist. Caliban for nine months of the year is Tartuffe for the other three.

One should so live that one becomes a form of fiction. To be a fact is to be a failure.

Moralists spend their lives in warning people against the sins of which they have grown tired. The active moralist is a tired Hedonist. At least, he should be.

A great romance is the privilege of people who have absolutely nothing to do. That is the use of the idle classes in a country.

Pathos leaves the artist unmoved. But Beauty, real Beauty, can fill his eyes with tears.

It is a vulgar error to suppose that America was ever discovered. It was merely detected.

One can always be kind to people about whom one cares nothing. That is why English family life is so pleasant.

In the well-thumbed lexicon of the journalist there is no such word as success.

Religions die when they are proved to be true. Science is the débris of dead religions.

People nowadays are so superficial that they cannot understand the philosophy of the superficial.

One cannot be too careful in the choice of either one's button-hole or one's enemies.

Perhaps nobody knows as I do what he [Oscar] had done for the 'new culture' [i.e. homosexuality], the people he has pulled out of the fire, and 'seen through' things not only with money, but by sticking to them when other people wouldn't speak to them. He is the most chivalrous friend in the world, he is the only man I know who would have the courage to put his arm on the shoulder of an ex-convict and walk down Piccadilly with him, and combine with that the wit and the personality to carry it off so well that nobody would mind.

— *Lord Alfred Douglas to Charles Kains-Jackson,*
10 September 1893

The only other occasion was a discussion about the word 'have' as a description of the sexual act. I said that neither the man nor the woman, though temporarily united, remained other than separate and distinct . . . He didn't agree with me at all. He said that the word 'have' was a perfect description of the possession that a man took of the woman in the sexual act, and discoursed about it, but not, to me, convincingly . . . I've forgotten entirely what he said.

— R.H. Sherard to A.J.A. Symons, 3 June 1937

Wilde told of me how, when he had paid a blackmailer £400 for a packet of his letters, 'I threw them into the grate, and, in order to punish the hands that had written them, I held them close to the bars, and they grew quite cold because there was no fire in the grate.'

—— *John Fothergill*, An Innkeeper's Diary (*1938*)

Dined at the Savoy tonight with O.W., meeting Sir E. Sebright and A.R. We sat from a little after 8 up to 11 over dinner but I did not notice the time a bit, such is the charm of O's conversation. He is such a puzzle to me, born it would seem, a teacher, he either cannot or will not give the key to his philosophy, and till I get it I can't understand him. He seems to have no purpose and I am all purpose. Apparently of an elegant refined nature, and talented as few men are, brilliant as a shining jewel, yet he teaches many things which cannot be held, and which are so false as not even to be dangerous. Well, I shall find out in time, no one can conceal their real nature for ever, meanwhile we have one thing in common which covers a whole multitude of differences.

— *George Ives, MS diary, 15 October 1893*

He wears a Scotch gray coat that reaches to his knees. On the little finger of his left hand are four rings, extending to the nail. On his arm is a gold chain bracelet with a heart-shaped locket. His sleeves are large; so are his kinked cuffs. His face is stoutish; it looks healthy but not ruddy. After the fashion of Cleopatra he lounges.

— Dramatic Mirror, *March 1894*

I have never known anything but good of O, and for years have received unfailing kindness & courtesy from him – 'kindness' because he knew how I loved to hear him talk, and whenever he came he poured out for me his lordly tales & brilliant paradoxes without stint and without reserve. He gave me of his best, intellectually, and that was a kindness so great in a man so immeasurably my superior that I shall always be grateful for it.

— *Adela Schuster to More Adey, 13 August 1896*

The advantage in my doing your play [*A Woman of No Importance*, in America] would be this, that it would be properly staged and dressed & have the atmosphere of good society that is so vital to a play dealing with the life of today. The so-called society plays staged by our best managers (I except Mr Daly) are grotesque, & the heroines are usually done by ladies whose idea of Society has been chiefly gathered from 'hops' at Saratoga & Long Branch. I can recall no instance in which a play of modern society has been properly staged in New York for the past 10 years – except *Peril* as mounted & played by Mrs Langtry. 'The Dancing Girl', 'The Idler', 'Lady Bountiful' were *all* without exception utterly ridiculous if judged by any one cognizant of the life they were trying to portray.

Now the disadvantage of your dealing with me is this – I can pay no advance *at present*, until I see how my present season turns out.

— *Elsie de Wolfe to Oscar Wilde, summer 1892*

Lord Caversham. Tom, how old are you?

Lord Goring. I'm forty-five, Father. But my best friends tell me I don't look a day more than forty-six, so you see I must have been living a very respectable life.

Lord Caversham. Well, Tom, you have got to get married.

Lord Goring. Married, Father?

Lord Caversham. Yes, Tom.

Lord Goring. I don't think I'd enjoy that.

Lord Caversham. My dear boy, when I was your age I had been twice divorced and was paying addresses to your sainted mother.

. . .

Lord Caversham. Too many books, Sir: a man of fashion shouldn't know too much.

Lord Goring. But I am not a man of fashion, Father.

Lord Caversham. More's the pity, Sir . . . I regard you as a failure.

Lord Goring. Everybody is a success nowadays, Father. It's rather vulgar being a success — I prefer being a failure.

Lord Caversham. Don't marry an American — American women are always cleverer than their husbands — and that doesn't look well — makes a man an ass.

. . .

Lord Caversham. I've come to take you to Lady Hartlock's.

Lord Goring. I can't possibly go tonight, Father.

Lord Caversham. Nonsense . . . You must show yourself there, Tom. Everyone is going.

Lord Goring. But I don't like Lady H.

Lord Caversham. Like her? Of course not. Horrid woman. Can't stand her. Neither can Hartlock.

Lord Goring. Then stay. I have got to go down to the club.

Lord Caversham. Certainly not.

. . .

Lord Caversham. Obscure.

Lord Goring. Obscure? It's better than that — it's incomprehensible.

. . .

Lord Caversham. What book is this? *How the Poor Live?* This interest in the lower classes is morbid, Sir, morbid.

— *MS of* An Ideal Husband

Clause 4. You are to arrange for the production of the play not later than February the first 1895 and I am to be consulted as to the theatre and as to the cast of the play. It is understood that I shall have no objection to its being produced at the Trafalgar or Shaftesbury or Court Theatres but that I should object to the Avenue Theatre.

Clause four of Oscar Wilde's autograph letter of agreement, assigning the English (and Australian) performing rights in An Ideal Husband *to Waller and Morell, 20 April 1894*

Morality is quite artificial enough. It always has been artificial. Our manners must be improved. The age as Aunt Augusta says is painfully natural.

I like manliness in women. Women are so manly that manliness looks effeminate in men.

You can't make a fool of a person unless he is a fool already.

To enter married life with a man incapable of deception would augur ill for a happy future.

A woman should know nothing before marriage, and less afterwards.

I have never sowed wild oats: I have planted a few orchids.

You don't seem to realize that there are lots of people in the world who have absolutely nothing to do and don't want to be disturbed.

The husbands of beautiful women belong to the criminal classes: the husbands of plain women have married into them.

— You produce a false impression.
— That is one of the few pleasures left to one in life.

— She looks on me as a son.
— Women of that kind are extremely dangerous.

Men forget: women forgive: that is why women are such an inferior sex intellectually.

Most people nowadays are compelled to live within their incomes: it is a tragic sign of the times.

I don't know any Duchesses who could be described as the thin end of the wedge.

Leading a double life is the only proper preparation for marriage.

— *Notebook used for* The Importance of Being Earnest

Algy. Anybody called this morning?

Lane. The *wine merchant* waited in the hall, Sir, from ten to a quarter to one.

Algy. I hope you gave him an uncomfortable chair?

Lane. Yes, Sir. I took one from your own room. A Chippendale ... Your tailor also called.

Algy. Oh! That is all right. Tailors are gentlemen ... Wish to goodness someone would leave me a large fortune. Can't go on as I am going on now. It is ridiculous.

Lane (*arranging teacups*). It *is* very unpleasant waiting for a better place, Sir. I know the feeling myself.

Algy (*looking at him with an amused smile*). That will *do*, Lane, thank you.

> — '*A1*' *version of* The Importance of Being Earnest / Lady
> Lancing: *First Act, in Algernon Mountford's flat*

St James's Theatre
Play: *The Importance of Being Earnest*
Final Return
Thursday Feb 14th 1895

Box Office..................	£83.
Grand Entrance.........	£32. 4s.
Upper Boxes.............	£6.
Pit.............................	£18. 16s.
Gallery......................	£10.
Cash........................	£150.
Libraries...................	£6. 7s. 6d.
....	£156. 7s. 6d.
Advance	£72. 10s.
Money Owing	£24. 8s. —

— *First-night returns for* The Importance of Being Earnest

I can, however, in justice to my friend [the Marquess of Queensberry]'s memory tell you that the card-leaving was *not* pre-meditated. An interview was desired. My friend never expressed to me ... regret for the steps which he felt it his duty to take in the interests of his young son. But, being of a chivalrous and kindly nature, he, after the sentence, felt sorry for Wilde, whom he regarded as a ruined man; he said to me one day: 'I'm sorry for the poor devil.'

— *Richard Edgcumbe to A.J.A. Symons, 13 November 1931*

You've been *An Ideal Husband* in your tin pot way no doubt,

Though *A Woman of No Importance* was your wife when you
were out.

At least that's what the papers say, of course they can't be wrong;

They seemed to say that Oscar's fun was very, very strong.

He wouldn't mistreat a 'Lady', no not even Totty Fay,

But with the pretty boys, he liked to pass his time away,

Champagne and Chicken suppers, and he'd also give them pelf.

He was fond of manly beauty, he's so beautiful himself.

Chorus

Oh! Oscar, you're a Daisy, you're a Sunflower and a Rose,

You're a thick old 'Dandylion', from your pimple to your toes.

You're the sweetest lump of 'Boy's Love' that's been picked
for many a day.

Oh! Oscar Wilde, we never thought that you was built that way.

— *from 'Oh! Oscar Wilde, We Never Thought That
You Was Built That Way', street ballad, 1895*

I do not say that he always struck me as a man who had not a scrap of affection for anybody. He used to talk profusely about his 'friends' or even his 'dear friends', but with him that did not signify profound feeling. To all his friends he was a trial at one time or another. Robert Ross was devoted to him, but he had no illusions.

— *Vincent O'Sullivan to A.J.A. Symons, 31 October 1932 (Clark)*

From the railings of the boat, as she got to Dieppe harbour, I looked down upon what must be a great man standing alone and looking up. I had seen a photograph of this beautiful looking man and here was a huge and fat person in white flannels with a comical little red beret on top of it all. Rather vulgar I thought. My heart sank, but his sweet kindness put me right quickly.

After a drink at a restaurant, we went into the Cathedral [St Jacques]. Running down into the vestry was a fine and open staircase from an upper room, at the bottom of which was a well-made door. 'I think,' said Oscar, 'this is a charming idea, so that you can see your visitor coming before you say that you are in or out' – and more of this pleasant nonsense. We took a cab. Passing over a shaking and resounding iron bridge out of the town, he likened it to something in Dante's Inferno, and then with my ignorance I felt uncomfortable. I wish I'd never come. But he talked on; anything to put me at my ease, I suppose. He thanked me for Erman's great work on [Life in Ancient] Egypt. It was quite dark when we arrived [at Berneval] and the tree frogs were singing like millions of canaries. His chalet was in a row of others covered by trees and bushes. He stopped the cab at one of them and when they were penetrating up to it he said, 'I can only find this chalet at night.'

— *John Fothergill, unpublished memoir*

Everyone knew how Wilde amused himself. Before the trial, however, no one had been offended. Then suddenly these same people became hysterical and did not forgive him, Rothenstein, for visiting Wilde after he was released from prison.

— Journey to the Abyss: The Diaries of Count Harry Kessler, 1880–1918; *entry for 19 April 1902*

I think that his interest in social outcasts such as le petit Louis was part of his antinomian pose towards life. A good deal of it was also sheer good-heartedness. He wouldn't feel any possible risk of social damage to himself.

— *R.H. Sherard to A.J.A Symons, 3 June 1937*

One often wonders if Oscar was a real man, soul or person – or a made-up thing to catch the public – but, as often, I think of this sight of him [sitting 'alone thinking' outside the Caffè Aragno in Rome] & of another vision of his face – we were at a 3d. show given in the schoolroom [at Berneval] of a little French reciter – we were sitting at the ends of the rows each side of the aisle between us – & the poor little reciter-man shouted & screamed & squealed & sweated at his work & I looked across the aisle, and I'll never forget Oscar's profile as he contemplated him – pity, pathos, care, patience & understanding.

— *John Fothergill to A.J.A. Symons, 1931*

Will Rothenstein: 'But I sometimes feel so *ridiculous*.'
OW in a stage whisper: 'But, of *course*, my *dear* Will, didn't you *know*? All *real* artists *are* ridiculous!'

— *Augustus John*, Finishing Touches, *1964*

April 1899

My very dear Oscar,

We want you to come and stay with us. My husband wants you to come so much – fancy, Oscar – I am married! To such a dear person. You will love him. He is not intellectual & not good looking but a King of men. He loved me when I was a girl of 16. You met him once in our drawing-room but you would not remember. It will be dull for you here. There is nothing in the World to do – but I want so to see you again – to show you my house – a tiny house – but full of books. The smoking-room shall be yours entirely – tho' we smoke all over the house. Do come. You are the first person I have asked to my new home.

Will you come as soon as it is a little warmer so that we can sit in the garden – there is a lovely well – & a fish pond. Will you come the first fortnight in June . . . Let me know in your letter the name I hear you have taken lately. Please come. I will make you write here. It is such a healthy place – Come, dear Oscar.

Yours ever affectionately

Frankie (Mrs Harrod)

— *Frances Harrod (neé Forbes-Robertson) to Oscar Wilde, April 1899*

Hotel Marsollier
rue Marsollier
Paris

My dear, sweet, beautiful Friend, [your brother] Eric has just sent me your charming letter, and I am delighted to have a chance of sending you my congratulations on your marriage, and the good wishes of one who has always loved and admired you. I met Eric by chance, and he told me had been over to the marriage. He was as picturesque and sweet as usual, but more than usually vague. I was quite furious with him. He could not quite remember who it was you married, or whether he was fair or dark, young or old, tall or small. He could not remember where you were married, or what you wore, or whether you looked more than usually beautiful. He said there were a great many people at the wedding, but could not remember their names. He remembered, however, Johnston being present. He spoke of the whole thing as a sort of landscape in a morning mist. Your husband's name he could not for the moment recall: but said he thought he had it written down at home. He went dreamily away down the Boulevard followed by violent reproaches from me, but they were no more to him than the sound of flutes: he wore the sweet smile of those who are always looking for the moon at mid-day.

So, dear Frankie, you are married, and your husband is a 'king of men'! That is as it should be: those who wed the daughters of the gods are kings, or become so.

I have nothing to offer you but one of my books, that absurd comedy *The Importance of Being Earnest*, but I send it to you, in the hopes it may live on one of your bookshelves and be allowed to look at you from time to time. Its dress is pretty: it wears Japanese vellum, and belongs to a limited family of *nine*: it is not on speaking terms with the popular edition: it refuses to recognize the poor relations whose value is only seven and sixpence. Such is the pride of birth. It is a lesson.

Ah! how delightful it would be to be with you and your husband in your own home! But my dear child, how could I get to you? Miles of sea, miles of land, the purple mountains and the silver rivers divide us: you don't know how poor I am: I have no money at all: I live, or am supposed to live on a few francs a day: a bare remnant saved from shipwreck. Like dear St Francis of Assisi I am wedded to Poverty: but in my case the marriage is not a success: I hate the Bride that has been given to me: I see no beauty in her hunger and her rags: I have not the soul of St Francis: my thirst is for the beauty of life: my desire for its joy. But it was dear of you to ask me, and do tell the 'king of men' how touched and grateful I am by the invitation you and he have sent me.

And, also, sometimes send me a line to tell me of the beauty you have found in life. I live now on echoes as I have little music of my own.

Your old friend,

Oscar.

— *Oscar Wilde to Frances Harrod, May 1899*

OW. 'How sad life is. Women are only brilliant while they are young & men when they are bald.'

OW. 'A man's digestion is the only thing in the world as Capricious as a woman; So long as you don't know anything about your stomach you can live with it in perfect comfort but as soon as it makes you aware of its presence it is intolerable; after forty a man's stomach finally manages to be disagreeable — very like a woman in this respect.'

OW. 'And every power we possess is a source of vice. Every quality has its corresponding vice. Insight habitually gives one arrogance — beauty robs one of modesty, manners make one cold, love makes one selfish.'

FH. 'I believe you make yourself out worse than you are.'

OW. 'Of course I do: if you pretend to be good you are ignored because goodness is so uninteresting; if you pretend to be wicked everyone says you are posing — for wickedness is fascinating.'

— Frank Harris, notes on dinner with Oscar Wilde at Café Durand in 1899 at the back of his copy (inscribed by Oscar Wilde) of An Ideal Husband

The last time I met Wilde, was at the Rodin banquet in June 1900. There was something humble and contrite about his demeanour which distressed me. He took hold of my hand timidly as if he were afraid that I would not take it. This attitude pained me and I judged that his misadventure had crushed him.

— *Adolphe Retté*, Le symbolisme: anecdotes et souvenirs (*1903*)

Purchased: 18 Octobre:

    The Ambassador [by John Oliver Hobbes]

    Hilda Strafford [by Beatrice Harraden]

Purchased: 21 Octobre:

    A Child of the Jago [by Israel Zangwill]

    March Hares [by George Forth]

    Raffles, The Amateur Cracksman [by E.W. Hornung]

    Alfred, Lord Tennyson – 4 vols

    Colonel Starbottle's Client [by Bret Harte]

    A Protégée of Jack Hamlin's [by Bret Harte]

    — *Wilde's account from Brentano's bookshop, 37 Avenue de*
                      l'Opéra, Paris, 3 December 1900

He said to me once, a few days after he came out of prison, that the Catholic Church was for Saints and Sinners alone. And when I asked what Church was for the others – the respectable people – he said 'The Anglican'.

— *Reggie Turner to Thomas H. Bell, 1935*

Dear Father Cuthbert,

The funeral takes place at 9 o'clock on Monday at Saint Germain des Prés and afterwards at the cemetery at Bagneux, I believe a great distance off. If you would like to attend, I shall be so pleased. Many thanks for sending me the Franciscan Sisters [to watch over Oscar's body]. He was particularly devoted to St Francis and deeply read in all his life and literature, so it is very appropriate.

Sincerely yours,

Robert Ross

— *'Petit bleu' carte pneumatique to Fr Cuthbert Dunne,*
2 December 1900

I had naturally thought that in Paris, where there were so many English and American journalists, I was likely to find myself among a group of correspondents whom I knew, and that it might, on that account, being a woman, be wise not to go alone. So I impressed two of my own sex to keep me in countenance. But the abandonment which — if half a dozen loyal friends be excepted — marked the last years of his life, also marked his death, over which so far as the big world was concerned, there fell temporarily, the pall of absolute silence.

When, on entering, we three women took our seats at the back of the chapel, I was surprised to find it practically empty. A few men were scattered about. There were then no other women. Even after the coffin was brought in, followed by Robert Ross, Reginald Turner, and Lord Alfred Douglas, and a few men whom I did not know, the chapel still looked empty.

It was a brief, sad, depressing low mass, cold and formal, especially so, as few of those gathered there were Roman Catholics, and as a result no one seemed to have any part in the service, and there was no solemnity about it.

It was tragic to realize that this man, a poet of parts, once a brilliant figure in Paris as well as London, the dandy of dandies, this lover of the beautiful, this amateur of luxury, so few years ago known to all the great men in the world of letters and fêted even by those who did not love him, had fallen so low that only these few cared or dared to do him honor, and speed him on his last adventure.

— *Mildred Aldrich, 'Confessions of a Breadwinner'*
(unpublished autobiography, 1926)

There was a young painter who also loved music and had a grand piano in his studio, an old Erard still beautiful, but with some keys dumbed by time in the extreme bass and treble. He had little leisure to play upon it but he liked to see it there while he worked; and in an odd moment he would try and recall a tune in the middle compass.

This had been for several years, and the instrument had become such a part of his existence that he hardly noticed it any more, so well had it taken its place in his room.

Then he began to fancy he heard a note struck as he came upstairs, a deep note or a treble one, so faint he took it at first for his own whim. But when this had happened several times he began to wonder; and try to catch the intruder by tiptoeing upstairs and opening the door suddenly and softly. There never was anyone there, the long room was always empty, and the gleaming lid was always closed upon the yellowed keys.

He questioned his landlady, a good, sensible woman, but she had heard nothing, though she lived just above.

And then the faint notes came nearer and he even heard them while at work, though only occasionally and towards dusk. He would turn round sharply, but there was never anyone there; only the dark, gleaming wood – which seemed to him by then to smile at a secret that it hid. And once, just once, he could have sworn he caught the faintest echo of a laugh as he swung round.

It was Winter when he first heard the phantom notes, and as the days wore on towards Spring and the evenings lengthened, their idea began to haunt him, coming into his mind at busy hours and even disturbing the tenor of his daily life.

At once perplexed, charmed and harassed, he decided to spend several nights in the studio; had a comfortable settee installed and brought in a supper of fruit and wine.

The first night he dozed off towards the early hours of day, and was wakened by the light treble and the heavy bass. Startled, he let fall the book he had been reading before he slept; heard the heavy sound, and then all was still, until full daylight brought back the traffic of the streets.

The second night he tried again to keep awake – and again he dozed – and again was woken by the dumb notes' sound. And as he started up he heard the closing of the heavy lid.

On the third night he prepared coffee and poured into his cup some drops of a potent elixir from the East, guaranteed to keep the mind at watch, however heavy the body might be.

The hours passed, chimed by the silver sound of an ancient clock. He read, and watched the Erard in the mirror over the mantelpiece, carefully keeping his back towards it, having discarded the settee for a tall armchair.

And that night, when the early hours approached, he heard the piano open and the music come; and not only stray notes of bass and treble, but a lilting, heart-rending melody played out in the treble and the bass.

In a second he was up, and on careful bare feet was by the music stool, and bent over the open grand; and as he bent he saw the dumb keys come up and, reflected in the polished curve of the lid, the fingers which had pressed them down. And as they lifted he saw too the reflection of lovely hands, hands which, discovered, vanished, and in their disappearance he felt the phantom of a touch upon his cheek.

And then he was alone in the emptied room, now chill and cold and lit by lamps dimmed by the widening day.

And it was his own involuntary hand that crashed down the lid upon the silent keys.

— Story told by Oscar Wilde to Agnes Hughes, during one of his visits to the family of Arthur Hughes in the early 1880s. Written up by C. Hale-White, in 'A Tribute to Mark Rutherford'
(unpublished memoir)

I am going to do the little gold nugget story almost at once. The *motif* charms me. But *ought* I to use your plot as my own?

— *Charles Haddon Chambers to Oscar Wilde, late 1887*

I send you a very clever feuilleton by young Haddon Chambers called 'The Little Gold Nugget', which I think would suit *The Sunday Times*.

— *Oscar Wilde to Phil Robinson* (*editor of* The Sunday Times),
16 January 1888

The Little Gold Nugget

It was given to Effie to take care of. It was not a great prize, for it weighed only seven ounces, but it represented the only result of a strong man's toil for many weeks, and as nuggets go, it was considered by no means a bad 'find'.

John Archer decided that the nugget would be safer in his little daughter's keeping than in his own. There were thieves and lawless men at this new gold rush, as at all new gold rushes, and they would know of his prize. They would probably try to annex it. They would search all sorts of cunning hiding places in the neighbourhood of his tent, they might even creep into the hut at night, to feel under his pillow and among his rough bedding for the yellow earth that folk hated each other for. If he caught the thief he would shoot him, but better not to run the risk of losing his treasure, and so he gave it to Effie to put in her old work-box. The thieves of the diggings would be too cunning to think of examining such an improbable hiding place. 'You must take great care of it, darling,' said John Archer. 'It is for your mother.' And Effie stowed the little nugget away in a corner of the old work-box — which had been her mother's — under the cotton and the socks she was darning for her father.

She felt duly weighted with the responsibility. She knew that this yellow earth was of great value, for her father, leaving her mother, who was very delicate, with some friends in Brisbane, had come a long, weary way to find it, and she had seen his sorrow, his despair, as day after day he had eagerly worked with pick and spade without finding what he sought.

Having hidden the little nugget away, Effie came out of the hut to look round and see if anyone was near who might have seen her. No. No one was near who might have seen her – only Billy the Black: King Billy, the aboriginal monarch, who loved rum and tobacco, and who was chopping firewood for her. King Billy evidently had not seen, for he was wielding the axe with quite exceptional vigour, and if Billy had seen, it wouldn't have mattered very much, for Effie trusted him.

The little girl's reason for trusting King Billy the Black was somewhat strange, and is worthy of being recorded. She trusted him because she had been kind to him.

But Effie was only twelve. As the child stood in the broad light, her tumbled hay-hued hair kissed and illumined by the bold rays of the sun, and her round, trustful blue eyes shaded from the glare by two little brown hands, watching King Billy at his work, a flock of laughing jackasses alighted in a neighbouring gum tree, and set up a demoniac cachinnation. What made the ill-omened birds so madly merry? What was the joke?

Effie's trust? Billy's gratitude? They failed to explain, but their amusement was huge and sardonic. 'Drive them away, Billy,' cried Effie, and the obedient king dropped his axe and threw & faggot of wood at the tree, which stopped the laughter and dispersed the merry-makers. 'Billy tired now,' said the Black, grinning. 'Too much work – plenty wood.' And he pointed to the result of his labour.

'Yes, that will be enough, thank you. You're a good boy. I'll give you some tobacco.'

'Billy's thirsty.'

'Then you shall have some tea.'

'No tea. Rum.'

'No, Billy. Rum isn't good for you.'

'Good for miners, good for Billy.'

'No, it's not good for miners,' said Effie emphatically. 'It makes them fight and say wicked things.'

'Makes black feller feel good,' declared Billy, rolling his dusky eyes.

This last argument was effective. Effie went into her hut – her father had returned to his work – and poured a little spirits from John Archer's flask into 'pfconikin'. Billy drank the spirits with rolling eyes, smacked his lips, and then lay down in the shadow of the hut to sleep.

The long afternoon passed very slowly for Effie. Her few

trifling duties as housekeeper were soon done. The little hut was tidied and the simple evening meal prepared, and some hours must pass before her father returned. How could she pass the time? She had only two books – a Bible and a volume of stories for little girls, which she had won as a prize at school in Brisbane. But she was too young to appreciate the first, especially as, the type being very small, it was difficult reading, and she had grown beyond appreciating the stories for little girls, having known them by heart three years before. She would like to have slept.

Everything around her suggested and invited the siesta – the steady heat; the brightness of the light; without the hut, the distant murmur of miners' voices, which came from beyond yonder belt of wattle gums; the monotonous hum of the locusts in the forest; the occasional fretful cry of a strange bird; and the regular snores of the fallen king, who slumbered in the shade of the hut. Even the buzz of the annoying flies assisted the general effect and brought drowsiness.

To remain still for a few minutes would have meant inevitably falling. Effie felt this, and remembered the little gold nugget. If she slept, a thief might come and take it. And so she put on her hat and, forsaking the seductive cool and shade of the hut, went out into the brightness and heat.

Archer's hut stood on the edge of the valley, over against the foot of the blue, heavily timbered hills. About fifty yards distant from it, hidden among the trees, was a high moss-grown rock, at the base of which Effie had discovered the smallest and sweetest of natural springs. Thither the child ran – looking back often to see that no one approached the hut in her absence – to bathe her face. In a few minutes she returned, drying her face in her apron and shaking her wet hair in the sun. No one had come, but King Billy was now awake, and was slouching lazily off toward the bush. Effie laughed as she saw him – his great head bent forward, and his thin, narrow shoulders bowed. She laughed to think of his laziness, and that he should look so tired after such a very little wood chopping.

She was still laughing at King Billy as she opened the old work-box to take another peep at the yellow treasure, and to make quite sure that the heat hadn't melted it away. And it was quite slowly that the laugh died from the pretty eyes and mouth – quite slowly, because of the moments it took to realize and accept a misfortune so terrible – when she lifted the coarse socks, and looked, and saw no little gold nugget – saw nothing. Then horror and great fear grew in the blue eyes, and pale agony crept over the childish face and made it old, and the poor little heart seemed to stop beating.

Effie said nothing and made no cry, but she closed her eyes tightly for a moment, and looked in the box again. No, it was no illusion: the little nugget was not there – the first gold her father had found, which had been entrusted to her care, which was to have been taken to her mother – it was gone. She put down the box quite quietly and walked out into the day, but the sun was shining very strangely and mistily now, and the blue sky had grown black, and the trees seemed to move weirdly, and the locusts had ceased humming from fear, but the strange bird was somewhere near, shrieking brokenly: 'What will father say? What will father say?'

But as the child stood there, despairing, her sight grew clearer, and she saw a black figure among the trees, and she was conscious of a pair of dusky eyes watching her through the leaves. Then, only, she remembered, and she knew who had done this cruel thing: King Billy. And she had been kind to him. Effie suddenly burst into passionate sobbing. The black figure still hovered among the trees, often changing its position, and the dusky eyes still peered through the leaves, and the laughing jackasses flew down to the old tree again, and laughed more madly than before, laughed at Effie's trust – at Billy's gratitude!

It was ten o'clock, and darkness and quiet reigned in John Archer's hut. Over among the tents, behind the wattle gums, a few gamblers and heavy drinkers were still awake, and their voices, raised in anger or ribald merriment, might occasionally have been faintly heard from the hut. But Archer, who had sown his wild oats, was a true worker, and he had his little daughter, for whose sake he had built the hut away from the noisy camp.

Archer had come home late and weary, as usual, had eaten his supper, and gone to rest without, to Effie's intense relief, speaking of the little gold nugget. The child was afraid to speak of the loss, and she was not without vague hopes that a beneficent providence would restore the nugget during the darkness and save her from this great trouble.

For this she prayed very earnestly before she lay down to sleep. Or did she sleep at all that night? She never quite knew. But she thinks that it was then that she first experienced that terrible, purgatorial condition which is neither wakefulness nor sleep, when the body and mind are weary enough to bring the profound sleep which they require, but which the brain is too overladen and too cruelly active to allow, when dreams seem realities and realities dreams. It must have been a dream when she saw something small and yellow float through the tiny window on the ghostly silver moonbeams. And yet, when, having closed her eyes, she opened them again, it was still there hovering about in the darkness – less bright now, and with a pale yellow halo. But it faded quite away. It was a cruel, mocking dream.

Then was it a dream when the old curtain which divided her corner of the hut from her father's moved near the ground – bulged slightly toward her? She would be curious to see, and she lay still. From under the curtain seemed to come a thin arm, and slowly, cautiously, after the arm, a head with a great shock of hair. And the moonbeams that touched a face. I think they kissed it, though it was black, for they found in a black hand the little yellow object which had floated in the first dream.

It was all so real, so beautiful, that the child lay still, scarce daring to breathe lest the vision should melt away, and when in her dream came the voice of her father, with the words, 'Speak or I'll fire,' her lips refused to open.

But it was no dream when the shot came, and the Black King rolled over on the earth, dead, with the little gold nugget he had come to restore pressed in the death agony against his heart, where, too, was a little gold.

And the laughing birds in the old tree, startled from their sleep by the shot, laughed once more, wildly and madly, at Billy's honesty, but there was bitterness in their merriment, for their master, the Devil, had been cheated of the soul of a Black King.

— *The story (mangled by the typesetter) appeared in* The Sunday Times *on 29 January 1888, and was reissued in* Oak-Bough and Wattle-Blossom: Stories and Sketches by Australians in England, *ed. Arthur Patchett Martin (1888)*

The hero of the Fancy was a young poet, who had dreamed so often, and written such exquisite songs, about the mermaids, that at last – inasmuch as the dream-world was more real to him than was the waking world – he was convinced that mermaids there really are in the seas around our shores, and that, if one waited long and patiently, they might, by mortal eye, be seen.

So, day and night, the poet watched and waited, but saw nothing. But when his friends asked him, 'Have you seen the mermaids?' he answered:

'Yes, by moonlight I saw them at play among the rollers,' describing what he pretended he had seen, and describing it with such vividness and beauty that he almost persuaded his listeners into believing that he was speaking truly.

One night, after long months of waiting and watching, the young poet's lonely vigil was rewarded, and he did, in very truth, see the mermaids.

Then he stole, silently, away, and, thereafter, he told no one what he had seen.

— *Coulson Kernahan, 'Oscar Wilde: Some Recollections'*
(unpublished memoir)

He said that though Androcles may have been an early Christian slave he was also a dentist. A certain lion found himself suffering from severe toothache and consulted Androcles on the subject. The dentist advised gold filling for the back teeth and an entirely new set of teeth for the upper jaw or mandible. Later, Androcles, because he was a good Christian, was thrown to the lions or, rather, to a lion, and perceiving when the beast was let loose upon him that here was an old friend, approached him with joy, feeling sure that the lion would not hurt him, inasmuch as he had made no charge for the gold filling and the upper set of teeth. But the King of the Beasts had other views and promptly tore Androcles to pieces, and chewed him up with the very teeth which had been so kindly and generously supplied to him.

— *Lord Alfred Douglas*, Oscar Wilde and Myself (*1914*)

'In a theatre in America,' said Wilde, 'there was a young flute player who was gifted with extraordinary presence of mind. One evening some of the scenery caught fire and, as the smoke and flames began to rush into the building, the audience prepared to flee. Whereupon, with singular presence of mind, the young flute-player jumped out of his seat and, holding up a lily-white hand, cried in stentorian tones: "There is no danger!" In consequence of these words the audience kept their seats [allowing the flute-player to make his escape], and every single soul of them was burnt to death. Thus we may see how useful a thing presence of mind really is.'

— *Lord Alfred Douglas*, Oscar Wilde and Myself (*1914*)

Would you think well to ask him whether he could not now write down some of the lovely tales he used to tell me? Remind him of one about a nursing sister who fell in love with the man she tended, killed him to save herself from loving him, and was finally transfixed by a hidden dagger in a crucifix. (This is a very bald reminder, but it may recall the story to his mind) . . .

— *Adela Schuster to More Adey*, *13 September 1896*